Betty Rosness is unique. She is en.. , ... *eart of gold! The depth of her involvement in Santa Ba.... ..* .... *Her contributions to our healthcare leadership and her understanding of complex issues have served our community well. So, read the book and enjoy the story of one amazing lady who has given forward in extraordinary ways to make our world a better place.*
—Ron Werft, President and C.E.O. Cottage Health System

You cannot read Betty's memoirs without being moved and inspired to do what you can with the remaining days of your life.
—Anita J. Mackey, LCSW

An inspiring account of life that began in the rural heartland of America ... It is rich, fun and honest! A much needed reminder of what really matters in life ... I wish every teenager could read it!
—David Winter, President Emeritus, Westmont College

From humble Midwest beginnings to a U.S. Senator's Press Assistant, Betty Rosness put valuable lessons learned to building some of our most important community assets. Her life story is sure to inspire young readers.
—Judith Hill, Executive Director, CCC

Betty is a woman who has always cared more than most about community. The Carpenter's Daughter *is written in a very entertaining poetic way, giving the reader true insight into a community leader.*
—Tom Parker, President, Hutton Foundation

The Carpenter's Daughter *is a page turner ... masterfully written with characters who are survivors with grit, humor, and rock solid faith in their Lord, Jesus Christ!*
—Helen Jepsen, Executive, Kids First

As a former lawman, I could always count on Betty's positive outlook on life and her strong walk with God, even during the tough days. This is the theme of The Carpenter's Daughter. *Don't miss it!*
—Jim Anderson, Sheriff-Retired, SB County

The Carpenter's Daughter *is a treasure ... like a small jewel box uncovered in an attic trunk ... a true, entertaining book that will inspire young people to reach for the best!*
—Patricia Montemayor, Consultant

The Carpenter's Daughter

To Lynn
With Love – in Christ
Betty Rosness
July 24, 2012

Betty J. Rosness

Printed in the United States of America
by Wilson Printing
Published by Rosness Publishing

ISBN 978-0-615-37073-6

WHY ALL THE LADYBUGS?

The Ladybug has been my signature throughout my advertising career. I chose her because of her bright red color, her industrious nature, and her fierce attitude toward enemy insects … bugs who would gobble up our vegetable and rose gardens. The Ladybug is a direct and victorious adversary. She simply eats the enemy (by the thousands) and protects her own by exuding a chemical that smells so bad predators won't get near her. Now if that doesn't seem ladylike, it certainly is effective! I believe the Ladybug is the most admirable, exciting bug God ever created.

All Poetry, Music, and Lyrics written by Betty J. Rosness
Cover design by Donna Greene, Greene Design
Photos from the Rosness Family Collection
Ladybug Graphic by Creative Cartoons
John 14 Arranged by Adam Phillips
Consultant: Patricia Montemayor

My special gratitude to my daughter-in-law, Sheryl, who brought it all together.

Editor-in-Chief and Publications Director
Deja View … Digital Memories by Sheryl
Sheryl Rosness

Dedication

The Carpenter's Daughter *is dedicated to my five children:*
Melody, Michael, Randall, Melinda, and John
whom I love more than life ...

and
to my beloved husband
Hank
who fifty years ago, made our family complete.

Contents

INTRODUCTION

I have never felt the need to write a book … or felt I had anything noteworthy to write about! However, after my 80th birthday, six years ago this past March, I began feeling that "it's later than I think" and if I have any last words, I'd better put them down on paper … at least put some of my life experiences together as memoirs for my children and grandchildren.

As I started assembling the pieces of my life that I could remember, I began to realize that some of my dreams, aspirations, opportunities and missteps were being experienced by girls and women universally. I didn't want my story to be a "tell-all" tale nor words of hurt to anyone along the way, but I did want the words to be from my heart and accurate in every detail.

Since I don't imagine myself a gifted story teller, I have tried to express these thoughts in the same conversational language I would use in speaking to the reader person-to-person.

Good or bad, the choices in this account were all mine. Any outcome of joy and/or success, I contribute to God's grace and to the wonderful family I was born to. The title was the hardest part. I must have considered two dozen different titles, but when I finally stumbled on to it, I knew "The Carpenter's Daughter" was perfect! I truly am a product of a wonderful earthly father, Thomas Harrison Pyeatt (Harry), who raised his family in the hardest of times by the toil of his hands … a carpenter his entire life. He and my angel mother, Margie, pointed the way to my Heavenly Father, Jesus, who was a carpenter in Galilee until the last three years He walked this earth. Between these two carpenters, I have been blessed to have survived and prospered while looking forward to eternal life with both of them.

If this humble account of my eighty-six years helps but one struggling girl, one confused young couple, or one discouraged senior choose a path of hope and promise, I will have achieved my goal.

Betty
The Carpenter's Daughter

BABY SISTER ... GONE

I was hanging over the sill of the open window searching for my baby sister on the ground two stories below. Shirley had to be down there because I saw her climb up on a chair near the window just moments before. I leaned over just as far as my four-year-old frame would allow, but couldn't see anyone on the ground. My thoughts raced by—maybe our baby had toddled into the kitchen to see Mother. Daddy had just kissed us each goodbye before he left for work in his familiar overalls with hammers and tools hanging from their loops. I loved it when he picked me up in his arms and told me to "be a good girl and help Mother today." I especially delighted in the embraces of my parents. Even at age four I felt the obvious chemistry between them ... my mother, a petite beauty with soft, dark hair and my daddy, "the handsomest man in the world!" I knew I wanted to be just like Mother when I got big and marry a man just like my Daddy. They had both been born in little towns in the Ozark Mountains ... he, in October 1894, and she, in August 1902. Both lost their mothers when they were small children and were raised by their fathers with the help of grandparents and step-mothers. They didn't meet until 1922 when Daddy was in Oklahoma City working on a building job and Mother was on loan from the Phone Company in Springfield during the flu epidemic. Daddy had just finished his tour in the U.S. Navy where he served as a medic aboard the U.S.S. North Carolina. He made fifteen round trips from New York City to Brest, France during his tour. The couple met at a "social," and Daddy said he thought Mother was the most beautiful girl he'd ever seen. Mother was properly "disinterested," but he was romantic and very convincing. On February 10, 1923, they were married by Rev. Forney Hutchinson in the First Christian Church of Oklahoma City.

THE CARPENTER'S DAUGHTER

Climbing down from the chair, I ran to the kitchen, "Shirley's gone. She went out the window!" Even then, I hated telling Mother because emergencies always upset her so much. Thinking about it in later years, it all ran together in my mind … a blur of terror and fear with Mother crying for help, running downstairs to get the neighbors to call for help, followed by sounds of sirens and people gathering around the small body of the unconscious two-year-old. A nurse, who was driving by, saw the gathering crowd and stopped to help. She held our baby over her shoulder to keep Shirley from choking on her own blood. I heard that the ambulance was in an accident on the way to the hospital.

I could only look up at my parents with a tight grip on Daddy's overalls, taking in the pain and knowing for sure, this was one of the most tragic, scary moments I would ever experience.

Many of these details I learned secondhand, but discovering the disappearance of my precious baby sister was an experience I had all by myself! Mother called Uncle Jake to find Daddy at the house where he was working. He wasn't really my uncle, but he and Aunt Marie were my parents' best friends, and it was not acceptable for children to call close family friends by their first names and much too formal to use "Mr. and Mrs."

I remember when Daddy walked into our upstairs apartment. He and Mother melted in each other's arms with Mother sobbing and Daddy trying to comfort and quiet her. I could only look up at my parents with a tight grip on Daddy's overalls, taking in their pain and knowing for sure, this was one of the most tragic, scary moments I would ever experience.

It was 1928, just a year before the big crash, and long before health insurance and wonder drugs. The hospital officials took a "promise to pay" from my father and without delay, admitted our critically wounded baby. She remained in a coma at least twenty-four hours. Daddy told us later that they weren't supposed to let him stay by her bedside, but he refused to leave, and they made an exception. It was a good thing because my daddy could become very determined when it came to protecting his family!

Hour after hour he gazed at Shirley's beautiful little heart-shaped face, praying softly for his baby's return. He didn't say so, but I knew that Daddy cried. Very early the second morning, Daddy was sleeping with his head on the railing of Shirley's bed, when he felt a tiny hand on his face. He jerked awake as she spoke, "Daddy, can I play with your watch?" It was always a special treat for one of his daughters to hold his prized pocket watch. "Oh yes, honey, you can play with Daddy's watch. Praise God for opening your beautiful brown eyes!"

There would be other times that I would fear for my little sister, times when I would feel she needed my protection, but nothing like our near loss in 1928!

My Mother

When I was a child, all wrapped up in me,
I thought I was the reason she happened to be.
Who else could make my days so right
From breakfast call to my prayers at night?
Tend the house, iron my clothes
Or kiss my tears away …
Tell me a story or sing me to sleep
At the end of her busy day?
Mother was mine, or so to me it seemed.
I knew not then, as I know now,
How my dear mother dreamed.
Dreamed of places she'd never see
Dreamed of things she'd like to be,
Longing for a world she'd never know
Living each day like dreams were so.
What poetry, music and color inside –
Glamorous roles she'd never confide.
Words can't describe my mother's heart,
On a dark day of grief, her world fell apart.
Then a bright day of joy
Saw her heart take wings.
Why did I fail to understand these things?
Did I have to become a mother to see
That my mother's dreams belong to me?

To Dad ~ With Love

I wish I had known a dear little lad
In Missouri long ago,
I'd kiss him and hold him, he'd never be sad
My dreaming won't make it so.
How can I tell of his work-worn hands
So soft on a child's fevered brow?
Or his funny jokes that made us laugh,
With his cares I wonder how?
When I had my firstborn, he held my hand
With tears rolling under his mask.
A man was not there … he took his place.
How often he was given this task!
A Frenchman of passion, an American of pride
A humble servant of God,
A temper for right, whatever the side
A Midwestern child of the sod.
Riches or beauty, what are they worth
Compared to the life I've had?
I'm the luckiest girl on the face of the earth,
I belong to a wonderful dad!

SIGN OF THE TIMES

Another sister, Eleanore, was added to the family in 1928 and a brother, Tom, in 1931. Mixed emotions attended these births because of the lingering economic depression and lack of employment in our country, particularly in Oklahoma City, the heart of the dust bowl. Scratching out a living was the daily torture of our daddy, and pregnancy, a constant fear for our mother.

Eleanore was a soft, bonnie little girl with a ready giggle, fair complexion, and silky blond hair (a throwback to our paternal grandfather, Peter Paulus Pyeatt). Tommy, the first and only boy, was a precocious and handsome child who showed unusual gifts, even as a toddler. I remember the day Tommy was born. Dr. Barker came to our house to make the delivery. Daddy told me to take Shirley and Eleanore next door to the grade school to swing and play on the teeter-totter. He explained that a new baby was coming to our house, but couldn't come with all of us there. We weren't too interested in being in on the event, not if we could play on the school grounds by ourselves! We weren't there too long when Daddy came to get us. With the biggest grin, he announced "you have a little brother." You would never have guessed, had you seen his face, that Daddy didn't know what we were going to eat for the next few days.

THE CARPENTER'S DAUGHTER

We lived in Packing Town, a few miles south of Oklahoma City Downtown where the sights and smells were to "get used to." We went to church at Exchange Avenue Baptist Church and got most of our emergency medical care at the Good Will Center across the street from our church. I will always remember with humor when all four of us children were taken into the Good Will Center for "mass tonsillectomies." Ranging in ages two and one-half to seven years, we survived this ordeal and were rewarded with ice cream and lots of "TLC." Tommy got double treatment just because he was a boy. No one had explained that while under the anesthesia for the tonsillectomy, he would be circumcised. This unexpected treat caused him to wake up with "Daddy, why does taking your tonsils out hurt your 'jigger' so much?" This painful but humorous question followed him all the rest of his life!

Somehow, being the oldest, I knew this was not all fun and games. As I pretended to sleep, I saw by the light of a lantern, my mother and father embrace.

The next summer the whole family took a most unusual camping trip. Mother's brother-in-law, Uncle Ralph, invited our parents to Springfield, Missouri with the promise of a paying job. He was building a house and needed a carpenter. We thought Uncle Ralph was rich, and I guess he was at that time, compared to most people. He was a realtor/builder and had held a couple of elected City jobs. Anyway, it was a job, and Daddy needed one at that time!

We had an aging Chevrolet which was loaded down with housekeeping essentials, clothes, and us four kids. There was virtually no money for the trip, but we took what food was left in our vacated apartment and scratched up over five dollars for gas for our three hundred sixty-five mile trip. It was hot on the dry, sun-drenched roads, and after a lunch time picnic, a long afternoon of discomfort, and an overheated engine, we had to stop. At dusk Daddy drove behind a big outdoor road sign and we set up camp. Pallets went down for us after bread and lemonade for dinner. We were all dead tired and my three younger siblings were asleep before they got their goodnight kisses. Somehow, being the oldest, I knew this was not all fun and games. As I pretended to sleep, I saw by the light of a lantern, my mother and father embrace. She was weeping, and he was assuring her that "things will work out." And, I knew that if my daddy said so, it would!

Early the next morning before we awakened, Daddy had walked to a nearby café and fixed some shelves for the owner in exchange for food. By the time we crawled out of our bedding he had brought us breakfast and put water in the car. We continued our adventurous trip to Springfield and enjoyed a wonderful dinner cooked by Aunt Myrtle, my mother's eldest sister. We spent that night in our relatives' beautiful home. We kids felt so pampered in surroundings we had only dreamed about.

I don't remember how long we stayed in Springfield that time, but after a season of work and pay, we returned home to Oklahoma City. We kids thought it was all a big adventure and were ready to go again at any time, but somehow I knew it was no picnic to our parents. I've never since been tempted to make camp behind an outdoor sign board!

The Gift of Life

Sometimes we wonder, "Is it worth it all?"
Life's disappointments, we soar and we fall.
We weather the storms and shake in the quake
Huddle in the dark until we awake
To sunshine, rainbows and the mockingbird's song ...
These fleeting joys don't last too long.
It's back to work, to battle, to climb
To dread, to fear and to grieve for a time.
You remember a promise, a rainbow appears.
In one magic moment, it erases your tears.
The tinkling of laughter, a special one's touch
Brings back the reason life means so much!

A Place in My Heart

There are those places and faces that come along in life that add a dimension that affects who we are forever. One of those places which defines my roots lies deep in the Ozark Mountains. My mother and dad were both born in the Greater Springfield, Missouri area. My grandparents on both sides were natives of this magnificent part of the world. Even the Great Depression could not dim its beauty and serenity.

In 1933, when I was nine years old, my dad's eldest brother, Uncle Rancon, and his wife, Aunt Estelle, visited us in Oklahoma City. During their stay, they made a case for "borrowing" me, the oldest of four, to spend the coming school year with them on their eighty-acre farm in Branson, Missouri. They pointed out that they had no children and that my mother and dad had four. My folks were reluctant at first, but persuasion and the promise of a once-in-a-lifetime experience for their firstborn won out! In looking back, I know this was a hard and selfless decision for my parents.

That summer I drove to Branson with my aunt and uncle and began an adventure that will forever be etched into my consciousness as a comparison to all other places and times in my lifetime.

Branson is just fifty miles south of Springfield, Missouri, and by the mid-sixties and early seventies came to be a celebrated center for western/country music and a major destination for family vacations. In 1933, however, it was a picturesque little mountain town bordered by the White River, Lake Taneycomo, and the Ozark Mountains. Farming and fishing were the main means of income.

Uncle Rancon was well educated. A WWII Veteran of the U.S. Army, he finished Business School and the School of Undertakers. He and Aunt Estelle, who was the only daughter of a Texas rancher, were married in Houston, Texas. My uncle owned a mortuary and my aunt helped run her family's restaurant in the City of Houston. As years went by Uncle Rancon became more and more disillusioned with big city life and felt a pull to the farm life he'd known as a boy in Missouri. One look at the farm

THE CARPENTER'S DAUGHTER

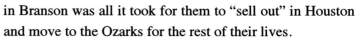

in Branson was all it took for them to "sell out" in Houston and move to the Ozarks for the rest of their lives.

What excitement I felt driving from Branson over a very rough terrain to the farm! I remember feeling scared when Uncle Rancon drove down a steep incline over large rocks and water and up again to the road. When we pulled up to the main house, I thought I'd never seen anything so beautiful! A white country house with a sitting porch, surrounded by stately oak trees looked just like the pictures of southern estates in magazines I'd seen. The rolling hills around the area revealed a barn to the right, a smoke house close to the back porch, a path on the left leading down to a fresh water well, and fifty feet further to a cold running stream used for the "refrigerator cage."

I was shown to my room and it was all mine! I remember that I had a little chamber pot for night use and a metal roof, which accented one of my favorite things ... raindrops on the roof.

It seems impossible now that a man and woman out of the big City of Houston found everything they wanted in an Ozark farm house that had no electricity, no running water, no gas, and no inside plumbing. I think they were excited with the challenge ... the challenge to bring back early day living while maintaining the charm and civility they both were used to.

I have come to believe that around age nine, one experiences thoughts, feelings, and sensations that are unequaled at any other time of life. I can still remember as though it were yesterday, the smells of the evergreens, the smoke from the burning bonfires, and the fried chicken on Aunt Estelle's wood burning cook stove. The wonderment of gathering eggs from the barn and the tiny, soft chicks as they broke through the shells kept warm under the mother hen's warm feathers ... churning cream, up and down, up and down until small dots of yellow appeared on the paddles and rich buttermilk is left behind ... gathering peas, green onions, radishes, green beans, and my favorite Ozark vine-ripened tomatoes from the truck garden. I haven't tasted tomatoes like those since. Maybe, because at nine years old, I was hungrier than I ever was before or since!

The name of my school was Oak Grove. Its one room held all eight grades. I was one of two in the third grade. My teacher was Miss Withers and she had to be well organized! There was a cloak room where our coats and overshoes were kept, and it also doubled for private correction sessions of teacher and pupil. Boys' and girls' outhouses were down two separate paths in back of the school.

On good weather days we all took our lunch sacks out under the oak trees in front.

I played the part of an angel in one production, which was strictly a cameo appearance ... but I felt so angelic!

I recall the delicious egg salad sandwiches (with a touch of mustard) that Aunt Estelle packed in my bag. The school was the center of our spiritual, educational and social life. Church was held there on Sundays and it occasionally housed a week long revival meeting. Traveling itinerate preachers took turns preaching. I distinctly remember one preacher exhorting, "Don't do as I do, do as I say!" Even at that time, I knew there was a poor message in those words. It didn't ring true to the Sunday School classes and sermons I heard back home.

Social events in the school house included Pie Suppers, where the girls and women brought in their pie behind a sheet and the males bid on the "shadow" and her pie. The highest bidder got the pie and the privilege of eating it with the baker.

At Christmas time Miss Withers directed a play which was practiced from the time school opened in September. I played the part of an angel in one production, which was strictly a cameo appearance ... but I felt so angelic! Aunt Estelle had made my costume complete with wings and wand.

I walked to school in all kinds of weather. It seemed to me to be about a mile or so from the house to the school, but a trip back to the farm a few years ago with my sister, Shirley, proved it was more like two to three blocks. It was a mysterious path through the woods and rocks. A couple of school mates who traveled the same path to school as I, made the experience more mysterious by showing me how to write messages in milk on paper, which we would leave in a hollow tree for each other, then rush home to brown the milk over the fire to read secret messages ... sort of like "texting" in the forest!

THE CARPENTER'S DAUGHTER

Aunt Estelle and Uncle Rancon would have made wonderful parents. They were patient and kind and always proud of each little achievement I made. Uncle Rancon spent many an evening after dinner with me practicing my multiplication tables. Every time I use that skill, I think of how many hours he drilled me with his hand made flash cards.

Aunt Estelle was an amazing woman, direct with definite ideas on everything. She had two personalities. One was a fearless persona in face of adversity and hard work. The other was a soft and feminine side with the ability to be a superb hostess, home-maker and "mother confessor." She could shoot hawks out of the sky with her .22 rifle as they circled her chicken yards for prey, or shoot the head off a rattlesnake on a wooded path. She was just as talented when it came to serving a company dinner … all from scratch, designing and sewing a stylish outfit, or arranging a wildflower centerpiece.

She was very careful to reinforce my own mother's teachings and showed me little ways that I could help Mother when I went back home. Folding clothes, drying dishes, snapping peas, and polishing silverware … all things I took great pride in demonstrating later. She said my evening prayers with me and kissed me goodnight. It makes me sad to this day to think how very much she wanted a child. She had no use for laziness or lying and didn't hesitate to point either out to the offender. Her straight talk limited casual friendships, but I don't think she cared.

"Which should I wash first while the water is clean, my bottom or my feet?"

I had many questions about life and change. She always answered them truthfully and simply. I remember one such question I asked while bathing in the wash tub located by the pot belly stove on a cold day. "Which should I wash first while the water is clean, my bottom or my feet?" "I should think your feet would be dirtier than your bottom," she replied without a smile or a second's hesitation. I was relieved that she gave me the answer to that heavy question. With many a bath or shower I'm reminded of her words.

On the weekends we drove into Branson to take eggs and butter to trade for flour, sugar, baking powder, corn meal, dry beans, coffee, and tea. Meats, poultry, eggs, milk, vegetables, and fruits were all produced on the farm. We even had our own honey from wild beehives.

A Place in My Heart

I shall never forget the sights, flavors, and aromas of that year. A wonderful couple afforded me a dimension in my life I would never have experienced otherwise. I've been able to travel to a number of states and foreign countries since, but the Ozarks still hold a special place in my heart, a place to which all other places are unconsciously compared.

Oak Grove Schoolhouse
Rural Branson, Missouri

BORN TO SING

From the age of eleven, I knew I wanted to sing the rest of my life! My two sisters, little brother Tom, and I formed a quartette and enjoyed the kind of close vocal harmony that sometimes happens among siblings. We sang at church and for revival camp meetings and it would sometimes "bring down the house" when Tommy, age four, took the bass lead with "down in my heart." Of course, being the eldest, it became my lot to schedule our rehearsals and teach the new songs to the rest of the group. This job became a nightmare that I could barely manage. Tommy was not a problem, but Eleanore, the youngest sister, always got tickled and couldn't stop giggling. Shirley was anxious to get back to a book she was reading and refused to sing the song "one more time." By then, Mother had to get into the act and threaten the end of our quartette if we didn't rehearse. But we survived and so did the Pyeatt quartette, during those childhood years anyway. By that time I was being coached by a dear Church of God saint, Mrs. Myrtle Dockum, our next door neighbor. She taught me my first solo, "Sweet Story of Old." We added to my little black notebook dozens of other religious songs through the next few

... the strongest ingredient was my ability to communicate the joy that was in my heart and mind to each person in the audience. There are few sensations in the world like that connection.

years. There was no greater joy to me than being in front of all those people in the pews, singing about Jesus and His love. It just felt right. My voice developed into a pure and pleasant medium range sound, but in looking back I believe the strongest ingredient was my ability to communicate the joy that was in my heart and mind to each person in the audience. There are few sensations in the world like that connection.

In 1936, I entered a summer competition at Rotary Park. Each Friday evening for weeks local crowds would gather in the park, sitting on the grass under the stars, to enjoy free entertainment on the stage. For twelve weeks, I sang "Melody From The Stars," "Treasure Island," and "When I Grow Too Old To Dream." There were contestants from ages eight to fifty. My entire family sat out there near the front row and neighbors had walked to the park with their picnic dinners to root for me.

I won the first night and stayed in the running to the last night. Winners were chosen by audience applause and my family and friends must have made the most noise. The last night of the competition, I was dressed in a white and red polka dot organza, waltz length dress that my mother had made for the occasion. I still have a picture of the skinny, big-eyed girl with straight, short-bobbed hair held back by two large barrettes.

I knew that I could not stop the music and extract the insect, so did the only other thing I could do ... I swallowed it, wings, antenna, and all, never missing a beat of the gospel message.

The Master of Ceremonies presented me with a wooden trophy imprinted with my name as winner of First Place in the Rotary Park Amateur Competition, 1936. Now I really had the "bug" for performing after my first taste of stardom!

I was to enjoy performing in song for a number of years, frequently as church soloist. One experience that stands out in my memory took place at the Oklahoma State Camp Meeting in Shawnee, Oklahoma. At the point of a particularly dramatic moment in a revival message-in-song, with my mouth wide open, a fly flew in! I knew that I could not stop the song and extract the insect, so did the only other thing I could do ... I swallowed it, wings, antenna, and all, never missing a beat of the gospel message. Only I knew what had just gone down ... of course, God knew! As far as I know, I never suffered any physical consequences.

Speaking of suffering, I recall my mother doing her share of that. She regularly called the kids in to hear me on a weekly religious radio program called the Faith Tabernacle Hour. She tuned in as the pianist was playing my prelude, which I knew at the time didn't sound right, but it seemed to be the right key, so I began trusting that she would follow. She did and I did. The only problem was that I was singing "The Nail Scarred Hand" and she was playing "The Nail in His Hand." I forged ahead hoping she would change her accompaniment to the song I was singing, but it never happened. I later heard that my poor mother turned off the radio two or three times hoping things would change in the interim only to hear me continue to sing my song and the pianist play hers. I'm not sure how long this duo tormented the airways but it seemed an eternity to me and undoubtedly to those who were still listening.

Fortunately, my love affair with music didn't die with motherhood. My oldest son, Michael, found his voice in junior high school when he won the lead in *H.M.S. Pinafore*. At Jeb Stewart High School in Falls Church, Virginia, he played the role of Curly in *Oklahoma*. U.S. Senator Robert Kerr of Oklahoma attended the premier performance. Randy, our middle son, attended every rehearsal and performance of *Oklahoma*. He was Michael's biggest fan and could sing the whole thing himself! Randy has sung ever since he was a small boy and at six years old claimed that he knew one hundred songs, and he didn't have to be asked twice to prove it!

Michael joined the Air Force Singing Sergeants in the summer of 1965 in Washington, D.C. and for the next four years performed with the group in a number of foreign countries. After the war he came home and enrolled in the Music Academy of the West in Montecito to study under the famed Metropolitan Opera Baritone, Martial Singher. In May of 1973, his graduate year, he was chosen to perform the lead in *Romeo and Juliet* at the Lobero Theatre. It was a great thrill for Hank and me to hear his beautiful tenor voice singing arias of love to the talented Soprano, Lois Vaccariello. We were blessed to hear him in several operas during our visits to Europe while he was under contract to the Darmstadt and Dusseldorf Opera Companies.

THE CARPENTER'S DAUGHTER

Randy, a self-trained Baritone, has filled us with song year after year, with his songs from the heart. He sings a lot of the old standards that I used to sing, but given a choice, his preference is to sing evangelistic hymns and patriotic favorites. His more than twenty year career as Executive Director of the Goleta Valley Community Center afforded him many opportunities to perform at Veterans Day events and on-stage Elvis impersonations. He is always willing to use his talents, free of charge, for funerals, birthdays, church services, and recordings ... all to the glory of his Lord and Savior.

My 80th birthday in 2004 was celebrated by the Channel City Club and guests at Fess Parker's Doubletree Hotel. The high point for me was when Randy sang, "You Raise Me Up."

My love for vocal music inspired the naming of my first child "Melody." I am so grateful that my aspirations for being a singer were carried on better than I could ever have hoped by two of my sons.

LOVE AND WAR

The years 1940 to 1942 brought more changes in my life than I could have ever dreamed possible. I wish I could say that they were carefree days of joy, anticipation and wise choices on my part. Only in distant retrospect could I see the blessings of my folly.

Yes, I was an above average student, excelling in music and English, but in reality high school was a blur of hormones, heartaches and horror. In my junior year, I knew I was in love forever with the only boy I'd ever dated. He had to be *the* one! We had been raised in the same church. His sister was my best friend … and I couldn't breathe when he was near. I know now he was never that carried away with me; but I loved him enough for both of us. And besides, my daddy never lied to me when he said, "I love you," and I was sure that this handsome, quiet boy from church meant it when he professed his love.

Ours was an on again, off again relationship, but my heart had been captured for good and no one could tell me differently. By graduation in 1941, the die was cast. We eloped to a nearby town and didn't announce our marriage for several months. By then we had to tell our folks because I was expecting our first child. Both families and our entire church body were rocked to their very foundations!

Melody, our beautiful little daughter, was born in November of 1942. Her father wasn't there for her birth. The pressure of his parents' disapproval and the prospect of fatherhood was too much for him to accept. During all this chaos he was drafted into the army. Melody became my whole world. She was symbolic of all the love I had felt for her father and all I ever hoped to have in a child. I was only eighteen but I knew that I would always love her and could never consider life without her.

THE CARPENTER'S DAUGHTER

My folks made room for us in their little home and with my mother's help, I went to work as a teletype operator for Western Union. I worked second shift so that I could take care of Melody during the day. Her father came home on furlough when she was just a few months old. He blamed his actions on his parents and asked me to forgive him. I did, though I was afraid he might leave us again.

The next few years were a nightmare … separations, reconciliations, tears, and unbelievable experiences of betrayal and heartbreak. On June 4, 1944, Michael was born, a big, tall boy of ten pounds! During the war we lived in Muskogee, Oklahoma; Cheyenne, Wyoming; and finally in Wichita, Kansas. February 19, 1947 Randall Lee was born, and on June 29, 1948 our youngest, Melinda Sue, joined the family.

By this time we had bought a small G.I. bungalow on  a bright corner across the street from a golf course in Northwest Wichita. My husband was a gifted artist and found work as a window decorator at a leading department store. His frequent absences from home and his new female associates led finally to separation and divorce.

My life, I thought, was over at this point and I wanted to die, but God wasn't ready for me to go just yet. Without monetary support, I was forced to put my four children, ages eighteen months to eight years, in the Wichita Children's Home, a facility for

children in family transition. I rented a room nearby so that I could visit them often and take them out on weekends.

I worked full time at clerical jobs and waited tables in the evening, but still could not make enough in those days to fully support four children. The picture of my four beautiful children huddled together in the Children's Home reception room still haunts my memory. My purpose was to remind them each time I saw them, that this situation was temporary and one day we would be together in our little house. They were assured that I would never leave them for anyone or any reason because I loved them more than anything in the world.

Two years later, I began receiving letters from my ex-husband ... letters of remorse and requests for forgiveness ... letters of professed love for me and for the children.

Now in Oakland, California, he was employed by a large and exclusive department store and lived in an elegant guest house for single professionals. He wrote about the good life in California and how much he wanted to share all this with us. He urged me to sell my house in Wichita so that we could look for a house to buy in Oakland. He further proposed that I travel to California where we could re-marry, and after we were settled, we could move the children to Oakland.

I knew there was very little trust on my side, but after careful consideration, I decided it was a risk I had to take for my children.

Everyone advised me against this plan ... my parents, my pastor, my lawyer, and my best friends. I knew there was very little trust on my side, but after careful consideration, I decided it was a risk I had to take for my children. Without help I knew it would take a long time to be able to have my family back together.

I talked it over with the kids and of course, with my parents. Melody was doubtful, the boys were all for going to California, and of course, Melinda, then about three and one-half, was noncommittal. My mother was dead set against the idea. My dad didn't say much, though much later he told me that he was very proud of my decision because no matter how it turned out, one day my children would know I went the extra mile to give them their father. So, California, here I come!

THE CARPENTER'S DAUGHTER

Michael, Randy, Melinda, and Melody

Michael, Betty, Melinda, and Randy visiting the
Wichita Children's Home in May of 2000.

A Guest House in Oakland

The train trip from Wichita, Kansas to Oakland, California was uneventful … many hours of watching the country pass by—which was an adventure in itself to a twenty-seven year old woman who had never been outside the Midwest.

I was met at the Oakland railroad depot by my ex-husband with a great show of affection on his part. I don't remember his asking about our children … maybe he did, but they weren't first on his mind. He picked me up in a friend's car and we drove high into the hills of Oakland to a large white three-story house. It was called a "Guest House" and was occupied by single professionals, both men and women, who had their individual rooms and were served meals in a spacious main floor dining room.

I was included as a guest for dinner and assigned sleeping space with one of the women residents. During the dinner hour several of the women made conversation with me. My former husband introduced me as a "friend" from Wichita, Kansas. One lady named Ethel asked me if I had any children. I answered "Yes, I have four," then promptly produced pictures. After that shocker, Ethel addressed their father with "Have you seen her children?" He looked stunned and was slow in answering, but I offered, "Oh yes, he's seen them. He's their father." With that, I had their undivided attention.

… I was a bruised but determined try-again bride. If my kids ended up without their father, it wouldn't be because I hadn't tried hard enough!!

But, I had come to re-marry this man and pushed any lingering doubts away. So, within the week, the license was obtained. Ethel and her fiancé, Fred, offered to be our attendants at the ceremony. We went to a nearby church parsonage and the deed was done! It was March 31st of 1951 and I was a bruised but determined try-again bride. If my kids ended up without their father, it wouldn't be because I hadn't tried hard enough!!

THE CARPENTER'S DAUGHTER

We moved into a tiny apartment across the street from the Guest House and I got a job working as a clerk typist for the Kaiser Corporation while my husband continued his job as a fashion display artist for a major department store.

In the six weeks that followed the wedding, we spent every evening and weekends shopping for cars. I had absolutely no interest in this activity and finally asked him why we needed a car when we didn't have the money to bring our children to California or to rent or buy them a place to live. His answer was "you don't trust me." I remember telling him that trust must be earned and that I had done my part by re-marrying him and giving him a chance to build my trust.

Before too long, I sensed a lull in his ardor. I knew the pattern by heart. We were making no headway toward reestablishing our family in Oakland. One Saturday, while he was at work and I was alone, I set out to find out just what was going on. He had a big trunk in which he kept memorabilia, including letters he'd received and unfinished letters he'd written. He had always had a problem getting letters mailed after he'd written them.

The trunk wasn't locked, so I began my search. I knew God wanted me to find the answers to my situation, and I did. One letter was nine years old from his father who reported the birth of our first daughter in Oklahoma City with, "Well, Betty had her baby, which usually happens after nine months." There was no mention of the fact that his son had anything to do with the birth.

Another letter was a recent unfinished letter to his parents, reading "I'm doing well on the job ... have met a beautiful and talented buyer at the store. She has a little girl and we get along very well!" The letter was dated a few days *AFTER* our wedding in Oakland. I knew then that he had not told his parents about our remarriage.

A third unmailed letter written most recently was to a friend in Kansas City, Missouri, and stated "I can't wait to see you guys. The old lady is here and looks like she's going to sell the house in Wichita and I can buy some wheels, so will be heading for Kansas City real soon!"

I knew then that someone back home was really praying for me! I had the whole story in black and white. My trip to Oakland was all a cruel hoax to get me to sell the house so he could buy a car and leave me in Oakland. He never intended to bring our children to California and our re-marriage was just a plan to get the only thing of monetary worth they had, a house to live in.

A Guest House in Oakland

I knew then what I had to do! I said nothing over the weekend to my husband about what I had uncovered. On Monday, I watched from our upstairs apartment window as the only man I had ever loved, walked down the sidewalk to the bus stop on his way to work. I knew then it was the last time I would tell him goodbye.

My heart was very heavy, but there was no turning back. I resolved that I would go home a different woman than when I had left two months before.

That same day I went to see my boss at Kaiser's and told him things had not worked out and that I must go back to Wichita to my children. He was very understanding, cut me a final check and wished me good luck. With that check, I did something I'd never dared do before. I went into the City to an exclusive women's shop where I'd seen in the window a beautiful all-wool grey suit. I bought it complete with a blouse, high heels and bag. As I remember, the suit alone was $85 and that was in 1951.

I walked on down the street from the dress shop to a high-style beauty salon. I turned my shoulder length dark curls over to a super stylist and said "change me." He did and I was beginning to feel "changed." With my fashionable cap-style hairdo, I returned to the apartment to pack. My new friends at the Guest House, who had quickly surmised the gravity of my situation, helped me get my bags to the railroad station and stayed until the train pulled out.

My heart was very heavy, but there was no turning back. I resolved that I would go home a different woman than when I had left some two months before. With the steady clanking of the rails I turned to look out the window and was stopped by my reflection. An unusual conversation began as the image began to talk to me!

Her: You do look fantastic, you know?

Me: I really hadn't noticed … before.

Her: It's time you noticed. I'm sick and tired of the way you ignore me.

Me: I've had a few things on my mind in the past few years.

Her: Yeah, I know … like "how could such a handsome, talented guy have ever married me?"

Me: Well, that has run through my mind.

Her: I'm not going to put up with your abuse of me anymore!

Me: Abuse? Just because I loved my husband, the father of my children?

*Her: You have brainwashed yourself to think you don't deserve him …
and I don't know why. Look at you!*

Me: I'm looking … I'm looking …

*Her: You came from a wonderful family. You're smart. You have talent.
You used to believe in you!*

Me: You think I ever could again?

Her: I know so and I'll never let you forget it!

That conversation with myself was long overdue but one I never forgot.

The trip continued and I became conscious of an Air Force Staff Sergeant across the aisle, openly staring at me. As our eyes met, I looked quickly away admitting to myself that I did look very "uptown" in my expensive new garb and my sleek, sassy hairdo. It also occurred to me that this was the first time since I had started dating in high school that I'd been conscious of any other man noticing me. Had I really let my self esteem sink so low? I promised myself then that on the names of my four precious children things were going to move up for us!

After more than two days on the rails, I arrived in Wichita without enough money to take a cab to my friends, Mr. and Mrs. Riggs' home, where I had formerly rented a room. So, I napped on the waiting room bench until morning when the buses started running.

My room was still vacant and I was welcomed with open arms but no questions. They took me to the Wichita Children's Home to see my children. I sat with all four

of them on the entry steps. Little Randy, age five, wanted to know if I was going to take them to California. Melody, my eldest, age nine, answered him with, "Don't ask Mama a lot of questions, Randy. Can't you see she's tired?" I told them that we were not going to California, but as soon as Melinda started first grade in a little more than two years, we were going to have our renters move and we could live in our little house and be together all the time. I assured them that I loved them with my whole heart. I would see them every week and would work very hard to make good things happen for us.

Who would have ever guessed at that time that there was a wonderful, loving man in our future who would, in just nine years, claim us as his and begin a brand new life in Washington, D.C.?

The Butterfly

From cocoon to bright wings in the glistening sun
Transformed new creature of God,
As you pause in flight, vivid colors one
With the rose and the goldenrod.
Life is beautiful for you as for me
Alas, it won't always be so,
When the storm winds break and winds blow free
Lovely butterfly, where do you go?
You're content to leave lovely memories behind,
To fulfill God's plan on your path,
Adding joy and beauty to whatever you find
Never mindful of the aftermath.
If I can but leave a bit of beauty behind
Soft and gently as a butterfly,
Perhaps, I too, God's answer will find
To eternity's unanswerable "why?"

A New Beginning
with Promises Kept

In the summer of 1954, I gave the renters in our little Wichita bungalow a notice to vacate. After a thorough cleaning of the inside and moving in some pieces of borrowed, begged, and used furniture, I brought my four beautiful children home to stay! Melinda, age six, would start first grade in September; Randy, age eight, would be in third grade; Michael, age eleven, in sixth grade; and Melody, age thirteen would begin junior high school.

Such joy we all felt, knowing we were together in our own house … well ours and Fidelity Investment's! That is when I knew I had to have more than two mediocre jobs. I needed a CAREER that would finance the household of five I was determined to house, feed, clothe and educate. There was no turning back now!

So, I started out with the billing machine at International Harvester to clerk typist at Beech Aircraft to the Security Assistant at the Air Force Plant Representative's Office at Boeing Aircraft Company. I made barely enough money from my Government job at AFPR to pay the mortgage, utilities, and groceries for some very fast growing appetites. I had no transportation costs because we had no car … no health insurance because there wasn't such a thing. Most clothing for the kids was provided by my mother, who worked in ready-to-wear at J.C. Penney's in Oklahoma City.

I'm so glad my eldest child was a girl … and what a girl! Melody was the most responsible and capable child I've ever known. She had mothered her siblings like a mother hen when they were in the Wichita Children's Home and they respected and obeyed her. After school and during the summer, Melody was in charge, backed up by Michael's muscle

and might! With job interviews, I always made it clear that I had to be available by phone because my children were on their own … and I can honestly say that privilege was never abused.

Those were simpler days … very little crime and neighbors you could count on. We lived across the street from a small convenience center. The pharmacist and the barber both kept an eye out for my children and were not afraid to tell me if they saw something that needed attention. It reminds me of Mrs. Clinton's book, "It Takes a Village." It certainly did in my case.

I had begun dating again … mostly Air Force Officers who had to check in at my security station at AFPR when they arrived to take the B-47 and later the B-52 flying courses. These officers were usually assigned three months duty at McConnell Air Force Base, located close to Boeing. The biggest problem with dating these officers and gentlemen was you never knew for sure if they were really single or not, and I had more than one bad experience on that score!

I remember that at one point I became so depressed and hurt by cheating fly boys that for six months I quit going anyplace except to work. My Michael went shopping with me one day and I tried on a very stylish dress that I thought would lift my spirits. I asked Michael if he really liked the dress on me. He very slowly answered, "I think it would look a lot prettier if you smiled, Mom." That convinced me that my six month isolation from men wasn't even good for my children.

In 1956, I briefly dated a young Lieutenant who had been raised in Wichita by a widowed mother. On our third or fourth date he tearfully confessed that he was married and this was the first time he had fallen. Since I wasn't serious about him anyway, it was easy for me to be indignant and unforgiving of his transgression.

A week or two after our parting, he called and asked me if I would like to meet a Lt. Colonel who had just arrived on base and was positively single. At that point, I couldn't have had less interest, but in order to convey to the poor Lt. that he was easily replaced, I said "of course, I'd love to meet him." I agreed that he could give the Colonel my phone number. Later, Lt. Colonel Joseph "Hank" Rosness called and told me that a young Lieutenant had spoken to him at the water fountain inquiring if he would like to meet "a real nice, attractive lady who knows Wichita well?" Hank never knew why HE was chosen, but I knew.

Some time later, Colonel Rosness called to ask me for a date. I had other plans but invited him to a local get-together where he could meet many of my friends. He rented an apartment about six blocks from my house and passed my house every day going and returning from the air base. He stopped sometimes on his way home to talk to my children playing in the yard. Our first "date" was accompanying Melinda to a Parent Teachers Association meeting. Hank seemed to really enjoy the evening … which impressed me more than somewhat!

Our relationship got a rather slow start, for several reasons. At first, I was otherwise occupied and not really interested in starting a new romance, so I introduced Hank to Jenny, a single mother of three. I would often see them on Saturday evenings at a local dinner club and heard from Jenny that she liked him a lot, but that he called her every Wednesday to ask for a date on the following Saturday … so, that wasn't going anywhere.

I observed that he was tall and handsome in a Jimmy Stewart sort of way. He was a quiet man, always mannerly and seemed to be sure of who he was.

Hank called me one evening to tell me that his best friend, an Alaskan banker, was coming to Wichita to buy a new Beechcraft airplane. He asked if I could get a few of my friends together and all go out for dinner and dancing. I told him I could do that, but I had a date with a friend who was in town for the weekend and I would have to bring him. My "friend," Frank, was an Air Force Major stationed in Albuquerque, New Mexico. Frank was a confirmed bachelor but I knew he was very serious about me and I also knew that he was very possessive and didn't appear to be good father material.

That evening at dinner, the Major got the idea that Hank was after me. I never knew why he thought that, as I'd never been on a serious one-on-one date with Hank. I had observed that he was tall and handsome in a Jimmy Stewart sort of way. He was a quiet man, always mannerly and seemed to be sure of who he was. The last time I talked to Frank, he stated, "I bet you marry that Colonel!" I don't know if Frank was psychic or just jealous, but his prediction took a long time materializing.

After dinner, several couples were on the dance floor. Frank excused himself to go to the men's room and that left Hank and me at the table. Hank asked me if I'd like to dance, but I declined. I don't know why, as I love to dance. Then I felt his hand covering mine as he said, "You should be with me you know." I saw no good reason to argue so I simply said, "Yes, I know." That was undoubtedly the most romantic conversation I'd ever had!

THE PROPOSAL

In July of 1960, I received a call from Lt. Colonel Hank Rosness, whom I hadn't seen since he left Wichita nine months earlier. At that time, we had an amiable farewell and he confessed his love for my four children and me. "I need to get away and see how I feel without you," he stated. He was comfortable with the idea of a bachelor apartment in D.C. since he'd been stationed there twice before.

As for me, I hid my sadness over losing the best man I'd dated since my divorce. After knowing Hank for four years, I had hoped we would one day be married, but as it hadn't happened yet, I gave it little chance of ever happening. He had shared his fear of marriage because he'd been close a couple of times only to be disappointed … and I'm sure he never contemplated marrying a large ready-made family!

During the nine months we were apart, he called often but I felt he just wanted to stay "friends," but this phone call was different. I really didn't know what was up! He was going to California to visit his mother and dad who were visiting his sister and brother-in-law in Isla Vista, a student village adjacent to the University of California at Santa Barbara.

I took one look at Hank's pale face and his Adam's apple climbing and falling and knew for certain it was the very best proposal this man could do.

"I'd like to visit you and the kids on my way to California," he explained. Not wanting to ask questions or give his announcement too much meaning, I agreed to pick him up at the McConnell Air Force Base Flight line. He asked me to make reservations for him at the new Schimmel Inn so the kids could go swimming He knew that would be a special treat with the hot, humid weather of Wichita in July!

The day of his arrival, I got the children in my little Ford sedan, after coaching them (especially Randy), on the rules for this visit. "You are not to ask Hank questions about his schedule, where he's going and when. He is our good friend. We will make him welcome but no different than any other good friend's visit. Hank and I are not getting married, but that doesn't make him less our friend. He can't marry anyone and you must understand that ... all of you!" I was sure I had made the rules very plain.

We picked Hank up on time and went directly to the Schimmel Inn. He had a beautiful suite and the first thing we did was all dive into the pool. After cooling off, Hank suggested that we order dinner on the patio, which was a real treat for the children. I do remember that I ordered spaghetti that evening. After dinner we were looking at a television program in his room when Randy piped up "How long will you be here, Hank?" His question brought a dirty look from his mother. Hank answered, "I thought I'd check with the Railroad Station and see what date the Texas Chief goes to Los Angeles. Betty, would you call them for me?" I obliged his request and found the direct route was on Wednesdays, information that I relayed to Hank. With the phone at my ear, I waited for him to confirm the reservation when he said, "Ask them if they have room for two."

In case the reader of this account doesn't recognize these eight words as a marriage proposal, I'm not surprised; however, all four of my children and I did recognize their meaning.

Melody, my beautiful first daughter, answered immediately "My mother's not going any place with you." Hank said, "Why?" "Because she's not married to you, that's why," she answered. "Well, I thought we could take care of that in California. Your Uncle Tom (a pastor in Inglewood, California) could marry us," Hank offered.

With the Railway Station Operator waiting on the line, I took one look at Hank's pale face and his Adam's apple climbing and falling and knew for certain it was the very best proposal this man could do ... so, if I wanted candlelight and violins while he got down on one knee, forget this one! On the other hand, if I wanted

to spend the rest of my life with this warm-hearted, honest Alaskan, I must make the decision now. I addressed the waiting operator with, "Will you make reservations for two?"

Randy jumped on the bed in his wet bathing trunks. "Mom and Hank are getting married!" he sang. My sales manager Bob Adams at KFH Radio Station commented when I gave him notice that I was moving to Washington, D.C., "That's the greatest sale you ever made ... way to close!!"

CALIFORNIA HONEYMOON

No, the kids didn't go on our honeymoon ... though some of them asked "why not?" We changed trains in Los Angeles and were met in Santa Barbara by Hank's sister, Sigrid, and brother-in-law, Bob Stearns.

My first glimpse of Santa Barbara was one of disbelief ... the Spanish architecture, picturesque shops, surrounded by the Pacific Ocean and wide sandy beaches looking out on the famed Channel Islands to the south and the Santa Ynez Mountains to the north.

We travelled through the city west about ten miles to the University of California at Santa Barbara and a student-faculty village overlooking the ocean called Isla Vista, finally arriving at a two-story four-plex which had been purchased a few years before by Sigrid, Bob, and Hank. The Stearns, then in their early 50s, were working for their degrees at UCSB.

After settling in and meeting Hank's mom and dad, who were spending the summer with Sig and Bob, we enjoyed one of Sig's delicious dinners and then outlined our plans for the next few days. We would have a very small family wedding on the patio of their upstairs unit. My brother Tom, who was Pastor of the Church of God in Inglewood, California (about two hours drive south of Santa Barbara), had already agreed to come with his wife, Esther and his little son, Mical. He would marry us and stay for the cake cutting and pictures. Note: Hank takes pride in the fact that HE made these plans ... all <u>before</u> he asked me to marry him.

I planned to wear a beautiful navy blue crepe coat dress trimmed in white appliqué, that I had bought in

I planned to wear a beautiful navy blue crepe coat dress trimmed in white appliqué, that I had bought in Wichita. However, the second day we were there, unexpected events would change my picture-perfect plans.

THE CARPENTER'S DAUGHTER

Wichita. However, the second day we were there, unexpected events would change my picture-perfect plans.

The next day Hank and Bob drove to Dr. Boots' office in downtown Goleta to pick up our blood tests. Meanwhile, I shampooed my hair and went out on the patio to dry it. I had never lived in a house with sliding glass doors, so when I went back into the house, I thought the door was open and proceeded to walk right through the glass!

With the crash, my new sister-in-law-to-be came running to find blood everywhere. Neither of us said anything. She grabbed a bed sheet out of a linen closet and quickly wrapped it around my leg. I don't remember any pain … only mortification and negative thoughts running through my head: "what could she possibly think of me? I'm getting blood all over her rug … what a mess after just meeting her."

Somehow Sigrid got me in to her little VW and to the town doctor … Dr. Boots, of course! While I was on the operating table, it seems Hank and Bob were still in the neighborhood and seeing Sig's car, came in to see why we were there. Hank told me later that Dr. Boots called him in to take a look at a nerve in my leg. Sixty stitches later, with my leg wrapped from ankle to hip, I hobbled out of Dr. Boots' office a pretty damaged bride-to-be.

My new physical limitations had to take precedence over the rule that a second-time-around bride never wears white. It took white to cover up bandages, so our shopping expedition the next day included the purchase of a white lace wedding dress in a waltz length.

We were finally married on August 5, 1960 by my brother, Tom, in the living room of the upstairs apartment on Del Playa Street in Isla Vista followed by cake and champagne on the patio. In attendance were Hank's parents, John and Helga Rosness, Mr. and Mrs. Robert Stearns, Rev. and Mrs. Thomas Pyeatt, and their two-year-old son, Mical.

After the festivities, Hank headed north to San Francisco

48

with his bandaged, but happy bride. The first stop was the Tides Motel at Pismo Beach. Following the Pacific Ocean route, I took in spectacular ocean views for the very first time in my life. The second day we arrived in San Francisco and wound our way through this world-famous city to the Fairmont Hotel, the grandest of all hotels.

We walked into the entrance of the Fairmont surrounded by marble floors, gold embossed mirrors and rows of flowers and palm trees. I felt a little under dressed in my Capri pants which mostly covered my bandaged leg, so I stood back under a palm while Hank went up to the reservation counter. He signed in and a bell hop stood by to transfer our luggage to the bridal suite. Hank walked back to "claim" me and we started toward the elevator when a voice called out from the registration counter, "Colonel, is the lady with you?" Hank had failed to check us in as "Mr. and Mrs." I was sure everyone in the lobby thought they knew what I was doing there!

But in spite of these mishaps, our stay in the bridal suite was perfect! I wouldn't have changed a thing. The mishaps only made our honeymoon more memorable.

My Tall Norwegian

May life not end 'till the answer I find
Where true love is born,
In the heart or the mind?
In youth we love
What appeals to our eyes.
But years have a way of lifting disguise.

I love you my dear for just being you,
Constantly near me, devotedly true.
I know your faults … I have two or three!
But no other man could understand me.

Your love for four, you took for your own,
The kiss you gave me for bearing your son.
The things you share with those I hold dear,
Will you tire or leave me? I have no fear.

My tall Norwegian, Alaskan by birth,
Man of compassion for human worth.
"Live and let live" cries your gentle heart,
Sensitive thoughts set your world apart.

You've no room for malice, no time for hate
And as usual with me, I'm a little late
In telling you, Hank, in words hard to find,
How lucky I am that you are mine!

THE 1960 INVASION OF WASHINGTON, D.C.

Hank has often recalled his 30-day leave in July/August of 1960 as one of the most frantic periods of his life. He flew from Washington, D.C. to Wichita, Kansas to propose. Two days later, we went to Santa Barbara, California by train to be married, followed by a three day honeymoon in San Francisco, then back to Wichita to pack, clean out my little house at 1402 N. Bluff, and buy a flamingo pink 1956 station wagon for the journey to Washington, D.C.

We piled trunks and suitcases on the top rack and the four children (ages 12, 14, 16, and 18) and our beloved Border Collie, Ace, in the back luggage compartment. I don't know what any of us expected of this trip or what we would find when we got there.

The kids were very excited. Melody had decided, against her best judgment, to attend George Washington University for her first semester of college "just for the experience" and to be in her new family from the beginning. Her heart (and boy friend) was at Kansas State University in Manhattan, Kansas. The boys, Michael and Randy, were delirious with joy at having a new dad and living in an exciting new world of glamour and plenty. Melinda was content if her siblings thought it would be fun.

As he walked by the reception desk, followed by me, four young people, and a Border Collie, the silence was deafening and the stares unsettling.

We arrived in Arlington, Virginia in the middle of a very hot August day. Hank had called ahead to the management of his high rise apartment to warn them of his new family's arrival. But, it didn't soften the shock. As he walked by the reception desk, followed by me, four young people, and a Border Collie, the silence was deafening and the stares unsettling. The kids could hardly wait to get into Hank's air conditioned apartment and into their swimwear for a dip in the pool.

THE CARPENTER'S DAUGHTER

The next few days we looked throughout the Arlington-Annandale area for a suitable rental and settled on a beautiful four bedroom house in a wooded area of Annandale. We had arrived! Hank was back to work. The furniture from his apartment was moved in and arranged. He ordered new beds and mattresses for everyone. We registered four kids in four different schools: elementary, junior high, senior high, and college.

I was very busy getting our new home in order and cooking meals for six eager eaters. I had always loved cooking even when I had very little food to choose from.

The honeymoon lapped over to these days when Hank would often bring home flowers from the Pentagon, a new habit I could easily adopt! I met several of his longtime military buddies and their wives. I felt very welcomed by them all. Some told me that they had long ago given up on Hank getting married. Several wives invited me out to lunch and fashion shows at big name department stores in Washington, D.C. We took in shows and dances at the Army-Navy Club in Virginia, enjoying such names as Tommy Dorsey, Harry James, and Nat King Cole. I felt like a queen with my handsome Air Force Officer husband, my beautiful home and daily experiences I had never known!

Then one day just a few months after our move, I received a phone call from the Administrative Assistant to Senator Frank Carlson (R-Ks). It seemed that the Senator had lunched with Mr. Tom Bashaw, Manager of KFH Radio in Wichita, Kansas. The Senator told Mr. Bashaw that he needed a Press Assistant in his Senate office to take over writing and producing radio tapes and newspaper releases for the press in Kansas. Mr. Bashaw told the Senator that he had an account executive, who wrote her own material and was Salesman of the Year in radio in Kansas. She had recently married an Air Force Officer who was assigned to the Pentagon and they had moved to the Washington, D.C. area. Thursday, the phone call came to me. I was pitifully non-political, had never voted and did not even know the political party of Senator Frank Carlson. I had heard his name since he had been Governor of Kansas and was in his second term as a U.S. Senator.

I promised to return the call the next day. That evening I told Hank about the call. I hadn't planned to do anything but make a home after I married Hank, but he said, "Think about it first. This is the kind of opportunity that many women come to Washington, D.C. to find. A job 'on the hill' is a chance in a lifetime!" I called the Senator and made an appointment to meet with him the next week in his office located in the new Senate Office Building.

JOINING THE U.S. SENATE

Senator Frank Carlson was a warm, personable man ... a former Kansas wheat farmer, one of five leading Baptists in the nation and was called one of the "outstanding statesman of the U.S. Senate" by author Theodore White. He was admired on both sides of the aisle for his candor, integrity, and wisdom. He hailed from Concordia, Kansas but lived with his wife, Alice, in a Washington, D.C. apartment while the Senate was in session.

He took me on a tour of his suite, introducing me to each of his staff. He said to each "I want you to meet the lady from Wichita whom I hope will join us as my Press Secretary."

How could I say "no" to that? He offered me more money than I had ever made before and gave me time to think about his offer. I really didn't need more time. My children were all in school and I could ride every day with Hank to the Pentagon and on to the Senate and back in the evening. It gave me a lot of private time to talk with my husband, an hour and a half driving time a day to be exact. Some days we had a lot of experiences to exchange between his job in the Pentagon and mine in the U.S. Senate.

In January 1961, the same day that John F. Kennedy took over the Presidency, I went to work for Senator Carlson. Every Wednesday after lunch, the Senator and I went by underground rail to the recording studio to record his message to his Kansas constituents via radio and newspaper. My schedule was very busy and exciting ... running into Congressional leaders whom I had only seen on television before. It was not uncommon to bump into the wife of the President or Vice President in the halls or waiting for a ride on the Senate rail.

THE CARPENTER'S DAUGHTER

Several highlights during the first year stand out in my mind ... one day I was left during mid-day at the reception desk. We all took turns at this post, while the

Senator and the rest of the staff were out to lunch. It was usually a very quiet time, but one particular day, a handsome man came in with a younger aide. He was dressed in a pin-striped suit and was especially cordial when signing in and requesting to see Senator Carlson. I explained that the Senator was at the Senate Barber Shop, but should be back shortly. I invited the two of them to have a seat.

> "Don't you know who this man is?" I glanced at the guest sign-in book and read aloud, "Sargent Shriver" with the same emphasis I would have given a "Joe Smith."

I went back to typing and answering the phone. I guess fifteen minutes or so had passed when the young aide approached my desk and said in a low tone "Don't you know who this man is?" I glanced at the guest sign-in book and read aloud, "Sargent Shriver" with the same emphasis I would have given a "Joe Smith." The aide continued with, "This is the President's brother-in-law and he is here to talk to the Senator about the Peace Corps bill." At that point Mr. Shriver walked up to my desk and assured me that all was o.k., not to worry, that he would call the Senator later.

I relayed all this to Senator Carlson afterwards and he never let me forget that mistake! Many times later when he introduced me, he would refer to that time with "This is my Press Secretary who is married to an Air Force Colonel, so when a 'Sergeant' called Shriver calls on me, she just lets him cool his heels!" He always ended that story with "I don't know how I've come this far with the help I have!" Note: Forty-five years later, I told that story to Shriver's daughter, Maria, then wife of Governor Schwarzenegger, when she was in Santa Barbara to address the annual Girls Inc. One Hundred Luncheon. She wrote me later that she had passed the story on to her mother, Eunice.

SENATE PRESS SECRETARIES ASSOCIATION

One day I returned from lunch in the Senate dining room to find a note on my desk. Barbara Bengtson, a prominent member of the Senate Staff Club had been in my office and noticed a picture of my brother, Tom Pyeatt, under the glass cover. The note said to call her, so I did. She had gone to Anderson Indiana Theological College with Tom. Since graduation, he had taken a call to the Church of God in Inglewood, California. She invited me to join her for lunch the following day. We had a wonderful though sad time talking about Tom, my only brother and the pride and joy of our family. Barbara didn't know that Tom was suffering from a malignant brain tumor and had been through one surgery to remove the tumor. He later had two more surgeries which gave him some precious time with his wife, Esther and their three small sons.

My contact with Barbara grew into a deep friendship. She was divorced and had one son, Britt. Her work in the Senate was noteworthy. She served two different Senators during her years in the Senate and was once named the "Senate Staffer of the Year." With several other Press Secretaries, she and I helped form the Senate Press Secretaries Association which I believe is still alive today, forty-three years later.

Officers of the new Senate Press Secretaries Association are:
Barbara Bengtson, Fritz Kessinger, Betty Rosness,
Chuck Bosley, and Grover C. Smith.

Our family often spent Sundays driving to nearby historic spots, e.g., Skyline Drive, a scenic drive through the Shenandoah Mountains, Gettysburg Battleground, Manassas, Bull Run, Monticello, and Williamsburg ... all beautiful to look at and rich in history. These were experiences that I never expected to have! On the return home one Sunday we saw a great number of cars around a small Catholic Church located out in the country about twenty miles from our home in Annandale. We parked to see what was happening. President Kennedy and Jackie were exiting the front entrance ... she was even more beautiful in person.

Pictured above are Reverend Billy Graham, President John F. Kennedy, and Chairman, Senator Frank Carlson at the U.S. Senate Prayer Breakfast.

THE SADDEST DAY in WASHINGTON

On November 23, 1963, I was shopping in Falls Church with a friend and neighbor, Sylvia Jarrell. I was in the dressing room trying on a beautiful floor length, white knit ensemble with little flecks of silver woven throughout the fabric. I had just told the sales lady that I would take it when I heard a lady shout, "President Kennedy has been shot!"

The place got very quiet and people rushed out ... wanting to get home and find out what was happening. By the time we got to the television, they had reported that the President was dead. The nation's capital was shattered! Going back to the Senate the next day was so hard. People from both parties were weeping and trying to make sense of the assassination of this young President. The Senator called me into his office to discuss what we would say in his radio address to Kansas about this devastating act. I remember asking Senator Carlson what would happen to our country with Vice President Johnson taking over. The Senator explained that the Presidency had a way of making a man want to go down in history as noble and honorable and Johnson would try to carry out the goals of President Kennedy, mainly Human Rights and Space Exploration. Of course, the Senator was so right. Johnson was able to get those things that JFK cared about so deeply, passed into law. I have always been thankful that I got to experience Camelot up close and personal.

NEW YORK CITY TRIP with the SENATE PRESS SECRETARIES

One of the great experiences I had in the Senate was a trip to New York City, May 6-9 of 1965. At that time, Ed Winge, Press Secretary to Senator McNamara of Michigan, was President of the organization and I was Chairman of the New York Trip Committee. Thirty-nine people went on the trip ... eleven of this number were spouses. We were hosted in style by famous names of the national press including: breakfast with Look Magazine, a briefing at ABC by Mike Wallace, followed by lunch at the Tavern on the Green. We took a tour of the United Nations with a reception in the U.N. lounge with the U.S. Press Corps including Pauline Frederick and Ambassador Stevenson. We visited the Fairgrounds and were hosted at a buffet-cocktail party at the World Wide Club. The next day we were guests at brunch hosted by Encyclopedia Britannica. On Sunday, May 9th which was Mother's Day, we were brunch guests of Boeing Airplane Company in the Terrace Room of the Dixie Hotel where we were staying. Would you believe that the rates in 1965 at the Dixie were: twin bed rooms–$15.50 per person and double rooms were $14.50 per person?! At the end of our trip we were given the grand tour of the U. S. Commissioners Pavilion and General Motors as guests of UNIVAC. We saw the General Electric exhibit as guests of G.E. I still have the folder with complete information of the trip and the many letters I received thanking me for the arrangements. I had a lot of help. The biggest disappointment was that Hank had to cancel as he was kept at the Pentagon that weekend because of a Dominican Republic squabble. Hank and I retraced the trip a couple of months later and took in some great shows on Broadway, so I got to go twice!

AND BABY MAKES FIVE!

Just before Christmas of 1961, I learned that I was pregnant! Hank was overjoyed, but at age thirty-seven, I was bewildered. After all, it had been thirteen years since I'd had a baby. I shared the secret with my girls and they were ecstatic! We decided to keep the secret from the two boys until Christmas morning. We wrapped some baby clothes and toys with tags marked "To Baby Rosness." That was the way we would break the news to Randy and Michael.

Michael, whom we called "Mickey" in those days, always played the Santa role, so when he came to the first baby gift, he just passed it off as a silly joke, but at the second one, he asked, "What is this for?" The girls started laughing and squealing, "Mom's going to have a baby." Michael said, "She can't … she's too old." I couldn't have agreed more. The next seven and one-half months went well with a couple of memorable mishaps. At about seven months I was delivering some official papers to another Senator's office. The marble floors were not planned for pregnant Press Secretaries, but luckily there was no one in the halls when my foot slipped and I went down stomach first! Only my pride was in pain, but I lay there for a

Of course, seeing a pregnant woman lying spread eagle on the floor prompted their immediate need to help.

few seconds praying that I could get on my feet before anyone came out of their office. It was as though the doors were glass, as several Senate staffers seemed to be in the hall at once. Of course, seeing a pregnant woman lying spread eagle on the floor prompted their immediate need to help. I was able to get up by myself, none the worse for wear. I have wondered since if any other woman ever experienced my predicament in the new Senate Office Building.

In my eighth month, the Senator called me into his office and advised me to take time off to get ready for the blessed event. He assured me that I could come back when

THE CARPENTER'S DAUGHTER

I felt up to it and work shorter hours if I'd like. I always accused him of being afraid he'd have to deliver my baby in his office!

One day shortly after I took leave from the Senate, Hank came home early and made the announcement that he had made an appointment with an Annandale attorney concerning his adoption of my four children. He surprised me as we'd never considered this option together. He shared that he had talked to JAG (military attorneys) and they advised him against adoption since we were expecting a child. Their experiences had not been good for servicemen who had adopted their wive's offspring. The imminent birth of our child was precisely why Hank wanted to adopt them. He didn't want them to feel second to his birth child. You can see why I loved this man so much!

He sat down with the children and explained what he was proposing to do. The boys were delirious and Melinda followed suit. Only Melody, who was eighteen by that time, expressed doubts and really didn't see her need to be adopted. Hank agreed that she should be given an option, because one day she would marry and her name would be changed again.

One night, I couldn't sleep and got up to find my husband walking the floor. I knew he was terrified because nothing ever kept him awake at night!

So, Hank and I and three of the children piled into the car to keep the appointment with the attorney. Melody came running out of the house exclaiming, "I don't want to be the only one with a different name." A few weeks later, after placing an advertisement in papers of the last known places their birth father had lived and notifying his parents in Oklahoma City, the papers came for each child to sign and Hank was the legal father of four and soon to be five!! This was undoubtedly the largest acquisition he'd ever made!

A few weeks before giving birth, the alarming news came out that a morning sickness pill, Thalidomide, was causing terrible birth defects, e.g., missing limbs and other body parts. This horror was reported to have begun at a military clinic. I remembered that in the beginning of my pregnancy, I had taken a medication prescribed by a doctor at a military clinic.

Hank and I didn't talk about our fears very much as we didn't want to alarm each other. One night, I couldn't sleep and got up to find my husband walking the floor. I knew he was terrified because nothing ever kept him awake at night.

AND BABY MAKES FIVE!

The time came one very early morning to drive ten miles to the Army hospital at Ft. Belvoir, Virginia. During my last visit to the Army doctor, it was agreed that I would have a spinal block, and on arrival I would be under the care of the doctor on duty, so I wasn't sure of anything. The doctor said that my obvious fear led him to think I'd never had a child before. I let him know that I had always known my doctors when I was a civilian and I'd never even met him before.

Hank stayed for awhile, but was told that it would be sometime before I delivered, so he went home to get the children off to school. I knew I was going to have this baby before too long, but was too occupied to object to them sending my husband back home.

Hank soon received a call at home that he had a nine pound eleven ounce son! They put me on the phone and I allayed his fears with the news that the baby was perfect and all appendages were intact!!

John Christopher Rosness was born August 1, 1962 to a family with four siblings. They each thought this baby belonged to them, and in a way, he did.

NORTH TO ALASKA

In June of 1965 the Vietnam War had the world's attention. It was the war everyone loved to hate! It was a time of upheaval in American society, rioting in our universities and tension in government and homes. It had gone on for several years with no sign of a cease fire. I remember thinking, "We can't lose this war ... what would the world community think of America losing a war? Why don't we just quit and announce to the press that we won and our boys were coming home?" It didn't seem to me that anyone was around to disagree.

Meanwhile, Hank was being transferred to Elmendorf Air Force Base in Anchorage, Alaska, an assignment that he had requested. Elmendorf was an important base in support of the Vietnam War. Their C124 aircraft moved the men and women plus their equipment into Vietnam and brought the wounded back home. Hank's parents were in their late eighties and still lived in Seward, Alaska, Hank's birthplace. Seward was just one hundred twenty miles south of Anchorage and that meant we would be close enough to see Dad and Mother Rosness often. This was to be a perfect tour of duty!

Our eldest daughter, Melody, married her college sweetheart, Richard Johnson, while we were in Virginia. They were settled in Oakland, California, where Richard worked as an architect and Melody as an Alameda County probation officer. Michael was in the Air Force Singing Sergeants and Randy was attending Kansas State University in Manhattan, Kansas. That left Melinda, age seventeen, and John, age three, to move with us. It was a very smooth move as the military packs and moves all household goods to the new base.

Johnny was crying for help and before I could get to him, Ace came from the back yard and had the Husky on his back with blood gushing from his throat.

The base was building new quarters for senior officers. We had been scheduled for one of the units, but had to live off base from August of 1965 for about three months until the buildings were finished. This turned out to be a very interesting experience!

I heard crunching noises after turning off the lights at night. Hank slept so soundly, he was never bothered, but when Melinda started complaining, Hank checked into the noises. The termites were chewing on the doors leaving saw dust piles on the floors. I sprayed bug spray inside the hollow doors and finally got rid of them.

We had brought our beloved dog, Ace, a Border Collie we had before Hank and I were married. One day, while Hank was at work and Melinda in school, I was getting ready to take Johnny with me shopping. I was already in the car and John came out the front door to join me when a large Husky from across the street got between John and the car. He growled and showed his teeth. Johnny was crying for help and before I could get to him, Ace came from the back yard and had the Husky on his back with blood gushing from his throat. A native Aleut Indian lady came running to rescue her dog and I turned on the hose to separate the dogs. The Husky lived and Ace was an instant hero. John still remarks about "the day Ace saved my life!"

Through mounds of snow on a frigid day in October, we moved into the new quarters. Our unit was a three-story townhouse with a generous living room, dining room, kitchen, four bedrooms, two baths, and a full basement. We were all fascinated with the laundry chute. We could drop dirty laundry from upstairs to the basement! Our car was hooked up to heaters in front of the quarters to guarantee it would start, even in sub-zero weather. I don't recall ever minding the cold or snow. I took a job as Marketing Director of Alaska State Bank owned by Brideen Crawford, widow of Hank's best friend, Ben Crawford, who was killed in his airplane returning from a trip to Seattle with his wife and two of their children, Ben, Jr. and Patricia. After landing in the ocean just off the coast of southeastern Alaska, Brideen and the teenagers were able to swim to shore, but Ben's foot was tangled in the rudder of the plane. Ben was a genuine hero in this tragedy. He ordered his family to swim to shore and promised to be right behind them. He never let them know that he couldn't get out.

Ben and Hank went way back … to birth really. Hank was born in Seward on May 27, 1919 to Norwegian immigrant parents, Helga and John Rosness. Ben was born in Moose Pass located about thirty miles north of Seward on the 29th of May to the

Drayton family. His mother died in childbirth. Ben was sent to Seward where there was a general practitioner who had helped in Hank's birth. Helga, Hank's mother, volunteered to breast feed Ben along with her own infant son, Henry. Ben often said that Mother Rosness saved his life. Mr. and Mrs. Ed Crawford, of Seward, adopted Ben when he was just a few months old. The two boys grew up in Seward and attended school through sixth grade when the Crawford family moved to Seattle. Through the growing-up years they stayed in close touch. The Crawfords returned to Anchorage after Ben's schooling.

Meanwhile, Hank was appointed to West Point in 1943 by Representative Anthony Dimond of the Alaska Territory. Hank had already attended the Diesel Engineering School in Portland, Oregon and one year at the Alaska University in Fairbanks, Alaska, when he received his appointment to West Point at age twenty-one.

After Alaska became a state in 1959, Ben Crawford entered the banking business and became prominent in Alaska politics. Many believed that he would one day be elected to the U.S. Congress, but his untimely death intervened. I give these details in order that the reader might know how these two Alaskans followed each other. The banker and the military man never lost their early ties. I first met Ben around 1956 when he came to Wichita to pick up a Beechcraft airplane. He was small in stature and his very poor eyesight required super-thick eyeglasses. It didn't take much time for me to understand why Hank thought he was the MAN! He was charming, smart, and in control! Everyone felt safe and happy in his presence.

I was so flattered when they offered me the job as Marketing Director which afforded me a view of the New Frontier that I couldn't have acquired without it.

After Ben's death in 1962, Brideen took over as Chairman of the Board of Alaska State Bank. Another very close friend, Dick Kennard, was President of the Bank. I was so flattered when they offered me the job as Marketing Director which afforded me a view of the New Frontier that I couldn't have acquired without it. Our daily lives in Alaska were exciting and invigorating! Hank was close enough to Elmendorf AFB headquarters to walk to work. Melinda took the bus to school and Johnny was enrolled in pre-school near our house. I drove the car each workday to the bank. We all wore boots and parkas nine months of the year. I wouldn't want to try it again, but forty years ago, I was in my element.

THE CARPENTER'S DAUGHTER

As Alaska State Bank Marketing Director, I made trips by air to Kenai, Fairbanks, Ketchikan, and Nome to visit the bank's branches. Each location was a story in itself ... spectacular scenery from snowy mountains to ocean glaciers and people who really cared about each other and the land. The first thing I did at the bank was to launch a campaign built around the slogan: WE CARE MORE. I was told that a caring bank hadn't been introduced before ... it certainly has since!

Christmas time on base was amazing. One holiday season, we attended twenty-nine festive events between Elmendorf and Seward. Usually on Friday after work, we headed for Seward, just one hundred twenty miles south of Anchorage to spend the weekend with Hank's folks, John and Helga. Johnny was their first and only grandchild ... and they couldn't

get enough of that little guy. Mother Rosness was a stroke victim and was confined to a wheelchair, but she loved to tease Johnny. We knew why we had come to Alaska when our three-year-old son would climb up on the arm of her chair to share a milk shake with Grandma.

There were some very sad things that happened while we were in Alaska. I got word that my only brother, Tom, would undergo brain surgery. I flew to Los Angeles to be with him and his family. It was to be the second of three surgeries he would undergo before his death in 1968.

Hank's mother died in 1967 after a brief illness. I sat with Dad Rosness in almost total silence while we waited for Hank to drive to the Anchorage airport through a snow storm to pick up his sister, Sigrid. We had a long, dark wait but I was so glad I could hold Dad's hand and just be there. He had cared for his beloved Helga for years with great tenderness and devotion. I knew his heart was broken. I sang "In the Garden" at her graveside funeral services. She was buried near her son, Jack, in the Seward Cemetery.

When Hank's tour was over in Alaska in 1968, we returned to California and he officially retired from the Air Force at Vandenberg Air Force Base. We had received news from our daughter, Melody, that she had cancer of the colon and we were very anxious to get back to California to be near her and my brother, Tom.

Hank chose Goleta, California near the University of California at Santa Barbara as our retirement home. He reasoned that the location was between both Melody and my brother, Tom, and we needed to be close to them. Of course, I agreed.

MENTAL HEALTH DRIVE SLATED IN MAY

Mrs. Joseph H. Rosness and Chaplain (Col.) Lisle Bartholomew discuss plans for the May fund-raising campaign for the Alaska Mental Health Association. Bartholomew is chairman of the 1966 drive and Mrs. Rosness is publicity coordinator.

Alaska is a chapter in my life I would not have missed for the world!

North to Alaska

North to Alaska, show me the way
North to the future, let me spend my days
Casting for salmon, panning for gold ...
I'll bag a bear and a caribou
And then I'll hurry home to you,
To help build Alaska, cities so tall,
Great Northern Lights will light the way for all.
Just a little bit north of the forty-eight
To the land of midnight sun,
Oh, Alaska, here we come!

(Sung to the tune of "Hey Look Me Over"
by the Air Force Singing Sergeants in 1967
for the Alaskan Centennial)

PERMANENT ASSIGNMENT

Hank had said for a very long time that he would like to retire in the Santa Barbara area and I was in agreement because I needed to be near our daughter, Melody, and my brother, Tom. Both were in the last stages of cancer and I felt I had to be present for the inevitable.

We arrived in Santa Barbara in August of 1968 and spent several days just looking at properties … mostly located near the University of California at Santa Barbara. Hank had chosen that location, hoping to take advantage of the educational advantages. We finally settled on a house on a quiet cul-de-sac in Goleta. It had a very large lot with fruit trees, shrubs, vines and lawn; three bedrooms, and two baths with room to expand.

Johnny saw several boys his age in the neighborhood and his school would be just a three block walk. Our furniture and household goods were soon delivered and we moved in to stay. Goleta was our kind of town! The people were friendly, the weather perfect and there was a rural, country feel to this "Good Land," which I learned Goleta had long been called. At that time we had four grown children … one married, one in the military, one in college, and one in the business world. Only our youngest son, John, would live with us and begin first grade that fall.

I just want to scream to them, "Can't you see what you are leaving out?"

After more than twenty-eight years in the military service, Hank was not quite sure what he would pursue but knew he wanted to keep up to date on world affairs while enjoying his young son as he began his education. I knew I would always be involved in community and family. And I knew that above all, I wanted our home to be founded on Christ. I began looking around for a church and finally chose one close by. Good Shepherd Lutheran Church was just three blocks from our house and only nine years old with a nice-sized congregation. I was looking for a place to worship that taught the Christ of the Trinity and a Christ of redemption. Also, I hoped it would be a church that my husband would attend and where we could raise Johnny to know his heavenly Father. I was raised in a Christian home. My parents were very active in the Church of God, headquartered in Anderson, Indiana. My preference in worship had always been less form and more feeling, but I reasoned that we could supply the feeling at home and in family worship. I knew I would be sacrificing my love of evangelistic music, testimony, and anointed prayer, but also knew Lutherans to have a quiet, steady faith throughout their lives … lives that often didn't express their highs and lows as did most evangelicals. I didn't intend to give up my evangelical zeal and thought perhaps I could share

some of it while soaking up some of the Lutherans deep-seated thoughts and traditions. I was proud that I was raised under the freedom of "no creed but Christ … no law but love" which had great appeal for me and still does. My little son and I faithfully attended Sunday school and worship services for twelve years until John left for college. I have continued calling Good Shepherd my church home until this day. My Norwegian Lutheran husband was never a great church attendee, but he always encouraged me and was glad I took Johnny to church every Sunday.

Hank and I became active in our Mariner's couples group and made very close friends through monthly dinner meetings in the church Fireside Room. We both loved our pastors and always supported the church financially. I have been blessed to have our wonderful Christian friends in good times and in bad. And, it was a wonderful beginning in Johnny's spiritual life. One of the saddest things to me is to see good parents do everything they can to see that their children grow up with the best education, the healthiest environment and the finest home they can provide, but neglect the one thing that is eternal, faith in our creator. I just want to scream to them, "Can't you see what you're leaving out?"

PERMANENT ASSIGNMENT

As for a career choice, Hank took a real estate course and joined Presidio Realty for a few years. He made some good friends and enjoyed exploring the housing areas throughout the Greater Santa Barbara area, but he always felt, after making a sale, that he was being paid too much for the part he played in the buying or selling of properties. He really never had the heart of a real estate salesman. However, he was successful in making some very good real estate investments for us and that was a good thing.

On the other hand, I loved marketing and sales, and since I had most of my experience in that field, I decided to put out my shingle. In 1970, I opened Rosness Advertising Associates.

So, I was off and running. While helping Goleta with their identity and SBNB get new accounts, I was introducing myself to the business community.

My first impression of Goleta was that this unincorporated area was viewed as the poor stepchild of Santa Barbara. As I looked over the largest businesses in the Goleta Valley, I found that the bulk of Research and Development Companies in the County of Santa Barbara were located in Goleta. Santa Barbara had made a shrewd choice in the early days by annexing the Santa Barbara Airport, which was surrounded by Goleta land and by name identification claiming the University of California at Santa Barbara. While those two large entities were located in Goleta, they were controlled by Santa Barbara City, State and Federal principalities. Large corporations, e.g., Burroughs, Santa Barbara Research, General Research, and Applied Magnetics lined the research parks from old downtown Goleta to the Timbers Restaurant on the west end of town.

Goleta wasn't claiming any ownership in this important business, probably because it had never become a city, but I thought it would help put Goleta on the map, so I named Goleta "R and D Center, USA." It had worked for the Silicon Valley and they weren't on the ocean in Southern California! I found a sponsor in Santa Barbara National Bank (SBNB) through the help of Mr. Harold French, Manager of the new Santa Barbara National Bank office in Goleta. By this time I was interviewing every sizeable business in Goleta to find partners in my venture. Mr. French advised me to call on Dan Turner, V.P., in their main office in downtown Santa Barbara. After I told Mr. Turner of my idea he said "This is just what we've been looking for. SBNB is new to Goleta and we're looking for new business out there in both business and individual accounts." So, I was off and running. While helping Goleta with their identity and SBNB get new accounts, I was introducing myself to the business community.

The Goleta Valley Chamber of Commerce joined us as did some twenty of the R&D companies. This was not a paying enterprise for me, but it was a valuable self-introduction to the area. We began with a "Gallery of Progress" featuring the participating R&D Companies with booths set up in the lobby of the new bank located on north Fairview Avenue. Each company chose a female employee to run for Queen of R&D. She would be chosen by votes of visitors to the "Gallery of Progress," bringing in many first time prospective customers to the new bank. The newspapers featured stories of the R&D firms and, for the first time, residents of the Greater Santa Barbara area learned what these companies researched, built, or sold. At the end of the month (October) a banquet was held and attended by all the participating R&D companies, SBNB officers, and Chamber of Commerce members. The Queen of R&D was crowned, with music and dancing to follow. The Goleta community gained new pride in who they were and the bank added hundreds of new business and individual customers. R&D Week was very successful for eight years.

Then the paying clients came: Rogers of Santa Barbara, Opportunity Shop, Gilchrist Jewelers, Trichler Optical, Harbor Restaurant, Mid-State Bank, Antioch College, three openings for the Bank of Montecito, Goleta Valley Chamber of Commerce, and America's Best, to name a few. I ran the agency out of my home office until Mid-State Bank named me Director of Marketing and provided me an office in the attic room of their Goleta office. I moved into that office in late 1971, sharing my work hours and weekends with my son-in-law, Richard, caring for Melody. She left us on February 17, 1972 in a fourth floor room at Cottage Hospital, surrounded by her family. It was nine months before I could begin to express this loss to our friends across the country.

Thanksgiving Day - 1972

My world is complete with the thought of her smile
Her courage has shown me the way.
Blessed were we who had her awhile
To brighten and strengthen each day.
God, teach me to love as she loved everyone.

PERMANENT ASSIGNMENT

Her selfless compassion, pray give,
Help me walk unafraid, 'till my task is done.
For the vision she had, let me live!
Live to tackle the jobs she began.
The wrongs she strived to make right,
A better world for her fellow man.
Please give me her will to fight!
The Lord has given and taken away,
But the girl will never depart.
I thank you, Dear Lord, this Thanksgiving Day
For the Melody I hold in my heart.

In 2005, Hank and I heard a sermon by a favorite television preacher of ours, Dr. Adrian Rogers. He spoke on "The Value of a Soul" and we were both so touched by the Holy Spirit through his words that we bowed our heads together in prayer and rededicated our lives to the Lord; that everything we did every day we had left, would be to His glory. We ordered five CDs of the sermon and that Christmas gave each of our children a copy along with the following letter:

Dear Children:

We have chosen to tell each of you this Christmas that we have recommitted our lives and purpose to our Lord and Savior, Jesus Christ! It happened after hearing the enclosed message on television.

We wanted you each to know of this decision and of our sure hope of heaven. We ask that you listen to the message and seriously ask God what His plan is for your lives. The desire of our hearts is to be with you all in heaven one day, reunited with our Melody.

You are the best things that ever happened to us. You have been wonderful children. We're so proud of you and so thankful for your love, always freely given to us.

Love each other, pray for each other and help each other along the way. Life is very short but forever is a long, long time.

Know that you have always been loved and cherished. May God keep each of you in His hand. Until that day …

From our hearts,
Mom and Dad
Christmas 2005

THE CARPENTER'S DAUGHTER

Hank, Betty, and Yogi enjoying their favorite spot ... Goleta Beach.

GIVING FORWARD

Every non-profit board needs someone on the board who has experience in advertising, public relations, and the written word. With my career experience I became a prime pick for board appointments. I tried to keep my board involvement to those things I felt most passionate about. Our daughter, Melody, had been a probation officer for young girls in Alameda County, California and held that position well after she was diagnosed with cancer of the colon. She had asked me to try to help girls find their way before they ended up in probation because "by that time it is often too late to help them change their direction."

She asked me to try to help girls find their way before they ended up in probation because "by that time it is often too late to help them change their direction."

After Melody's death in February of 1972, I looked for a cause that would extend her life influence and found it almost immediately in the Goleta Valley Girls Club (now Girls Inc. of Greater Santa Barbara). I joined the Girls Club Board and in less than three months was elected President. At that time the Girls Club was located in a little house on Pine Avenue in downtown Goleta. I was fortunate to work with Jan Roberta, a UCSB graduate who was the Club's first Administrator. She was smart, soft-spoken, and had large dreams for Goleta's girls! (Note: Jan spent her entire career with Girls Inc. progressing from Girls Club in Goleta to a top level professional in the New York City National Office, from which she retired a few years ago.)

One day, a couple of years into my Presidency, Jan told me that the Baptist Church building on Magnolia Street, a few blocks from the Pine Street location, was for sale and it would make such a great center for the club, but we had NO money. We had some very savvy board members, parents and business leaders, including Frank Bailey, Realtor; the late Jim Ix, Petroleum business; and Carnzu Clark and Perri Harcourt, local philanthropists. They were very capable of figuring out how to structure a good deal, but we needed a sizeable down payment. Jan had heard that the Fleischmann Foundation was dissolving their funds through distribution among non-profits. I was inspired to write to Mr. Max Fleischmann, Jr. in Los Angeles and tell him of our need. Very shortly thereafter, I received a call from Mr. Fleischmann, asking me to meet him on a certain date and time at the Pine Street Girls Club!! Jan and I were there early when a long, black chauffeured limousine drove up in front. Mr. Fleishmann got out and walked up to the front door. After greeting him, we invited him inside to look around. A group of young girls were in a class in the living room. In very short order he saw the problem … no play area, cramped quarters and no room to expand. I remember him saying, "This won't do. Let me see what we can do."

In less than a week, Jan called me with the big news. We had received a $25,000 check from the Fleishmann Foundation. We had more than our down payment! We purchased the Baptist Church and began renovation, with the girls watching it all. I had such a feeling of exhilaration. This was only the beginning of my love of non-profits and philanthropy … and it all happened because of my first child, our precious Melody.

For the next thirty years, beyond my retirement from business, I was consumed with board meetings and fund raising. This pattern was happily interrupted in the early 1980s with a call from a Los Angeles headhunter firm. They were not forthcoming in naming their source, but assured me that they were looking for a board member

for a very large and prestigious corporation. A lady executive from the firm called on me and asked many questions about my background, family, and present involvement. I remember telling her that my plate was full of non-profit duties and with a son about to enter college, I really couldn't take on another volunteer board job. She assured me that this opportunity would be "well paid" and that instantly got my attention.

A short time later, I received a call from Mr. David Tilton, Chairman of the Board of Financial of Santa Barbara, parent of Santa Barbara Savings and Loan. Over lunch, Mr. Tilton invited me to become the first

woman on their Board of Directors. Not only was I enormously flattered to be considered, but was excited to have this wonderful opportunity ... a privilege I enjoyed for nearly a decade. My leadership in the community and my background in bank marketing played a large part in my selection. I made some wonderful friends at Santa Barbara Savings ... men who were professionals of the highest order and they all treated me as an equal in every way. David Tilton's father, Lloyd Tilton, started the company in

As I wind down, I know that my greatest accomplishments are my children and I shall forever be thankful for the blessings I have had from giving them birth.

1887 and during my tenure as a director we surpassed one hundred offices throughout California. My job on the Board of Santa Barbara Savings helped pay for our youngest son, John's, college years at Westmont for two years, UCSD with a BA in Political Science, and the University of San Diego, where he received his MBA in 1988. I'll always be grateful to Santa Barbara Savings for providing some of my best years which I invested well!

I have been more than adequately thanked for my part in the betterment of Santa Barbara/Goleta through non-profit involvement. My dining room and office walls are filled with awards. My files are filled with letters of commendations and certificates of merit. I didn't do any of it to be honored, but have to admit that it feels good to be appreciated by one's neighbors, friends, and local officials.

It's been a great journey and on the whole, a very wonderful life! I have few regrets, though I do have some. For the ones caused by poor choices, I have been forgiven. For those that just happened along the way, I thank God and His earthly angels for helping me through those periods. As I wind down, I know that my greatest

accomplishments are my children and I shall forever be thankful for the blessings I have had from giving them birth. I feel their love and only hope their lives will be so blessed!

THE CARPENTER'S DAUGHTER

Listed below are some of the wonderful awards
I have been privileged to receive through the years.

Santa Barbara Woman of the Year — *1978*

UCSB Affiliate of the Year Award — *1984-85*

Soroptomist International Woman of Distinction — *1989*

Santa Barbara County Woman of the Year — *1994*

Santa Barbara News Press Lifetime Achievement Award — *1997*

Volunteer of the Year Award on National Philanthropist Day — *1997*

Goleta Valley Chamber of Commerce Golden Deed Award — *1999*

Rotary Club North Paul Harris Fellow Award — *1999*

Westmont Medal of Honor — *2001*

Cottage Health System Certificate of Appreciation — *2004*

Channel City Club 80th birthday recognition luncheon — *2004*

*Sansum Diabetes Research Institute's
W. D. Sansum Award for Service* — *2006*

Senior Citizen of the Year — *2006*
Central Coast Commission for Senior Citizens Area Agency on Aging

*Wisdom Tree Planting in my name at the new Girls Inc. building
Awarded by Girls Inc. of Greater Santa Barbara
and Goleta Valley Beautiful* — *2009*

Non~Profit Affiliations

C.E.T.A. Project of S.B. County: 1977–78

Channel City Club: 40 year member; Executive Editor;
Member Executive Committee from 1991 to present

Children's World of Hospice: Co-Founder

City of Hope, Goleta Branch: 1984-1985

Club West Track and Field: Founding member

Council of Christmas Cheer: 1970 Christmas Appeal

Dos Pueblos Little League: Founding member — 1974

Goleta Valley Beautiful: Founding Member — 1973

Goleta Valley Chamber of Commerce: Lifetime Member

Goleta Valley Girl's Club: President 1972-1975;
Helped accomplish the purchase of the Baptist Church
in Downtown Goleta for a permanent home

Goleta Valley Hospital: Board Member 1980-96; First woman Chairman;
Accomplishments: Goleta Valley Breast Care Center and first hospital to
financially support the Nursing Program at Santa Barbara City College;
helped facilitate the merger with Santa Barbara Cottage Hospital

Private Industry Council: 1979-86; Chairperson one term

Retired Officers Women's Association: 1970-2001 — President two terms

Santa Barbara Ad Club

Santa Barbara Cancer Foundation: 1982-88

Santa Barbara Chamber of Commerce: Vice President — 1980

Santa Barbara Cottage Hospital System: 1996-1998

Santa Barbara County Women's Health Coalition: 1999 to present
Board Member thirteen years; Chairman two years

Santa Barbara Scholarship Foundation: 1980s to present
Advisory Council Member

Santa Barbara Symphony: Vice President 1973-83

Save The Hospital Committee

UCSB Affiliates: Chairman of Board during 1980s
Accomplishments: the consolidation of 5 Affiliate groups
and produced the largest Affiliate fund raiser to date,
"Romancing the Stone" premier with Michael Douglas

UCSB Events Facility Committee: 1978

UCSB Veritas Forum: 2002-2005

Work, Inc.: Board Member during late '70s

PHOTO ALBUM

The Pyeatt Family

Mother
&
Daddy

Pyeatt Siblings
Betty, Tom, Eleanore, and Shirley

Tom 1931 – 1968

The Carpenter's Family

Hank

John, Randy, Michael, and Melinda
with Hank

Betty and
her children

Randy, Betty, Melinda, and Michael

Betty, Michael, Melinda, and Randy

Picture Left:
Betty with Barry Holmes, Pres.,
Santa Barbara Savings –
1978 Santa Barbara Woman
of the Year Award

Picture Below:
Betty with Robert Kallman

1997 Santa Barbara News Press Lifetime Achievement Awards recipients
Robert Kallman, Betty, Stuart Taylor, and Genevieve Nowlin

Picture Right:
Westmont Medal
of Honor

Picture Above:
Betty talking with
Vice President
Hubert Humphrey
at the United Nations

Picture Right:
CA Representative
Lois Capps,
Betty, and
President Clinton

Picture Above:
Larry Crandell and Betty

Picture Right:
Fess Parker and Betty

Picture Below:
Betty honored by Girls Inc.
Wisdom Tree Planting

SYCAMORE CLONE OF THE
HISTORIC GOLETA WITNESS TREE
PLANTED 11/6/09 IN HONOR OF
BETTY ROSNESS
WHO WAS INSTRUMENTAL IN THE CONSTRUCTION
OF THIS GIRLS INC. FACILITY. BETTY'S PERSEVERING
DEDICATION TO HELP GIRLS FIND THEIR WAY IN LIFE
INSPIRES HER TO HAVE ASSISTED THE YOUNG WOMEN
IN THIS COMMUNITY SINCE 1972.

GOLETA VALLEY BEAUTIFUL
GIRLS INC.

Betty, as a child, and Granddaughter Jannelle (pictured lower right)

SHORT STORIES

The Day My Mother Stood Up for Me

It was 1936 in Oklahoma City, between the Great Depression and WWII. I was twelve years old and in the seventh grade, the first year of junior high school. I felt so lucky to be in Mrs. Simpson's English class. She was also the school's drama coach and had a sharp, sarcastic wit that was so appealing to her students. Her daughter, Ramah, was in one of my classes.

I was a skinny, straight–haired, starry–eyed kid … oldest of four, who had dreams of being another Judy Garland. The day it all came down around me was exam day in English, my favorite subject! Mrs. Simpson passed out the test papers and gave the "go" signal, but I wasn't quite through talking to my friend seated in back of me. I don't remember what my friend whispered to me, or what my answer was, but I do know it had nothing to do with the test … just silly trivia between two talkative girls.

The only one of us that Mrs. Simpson saw was me. She called me to the front of the class and presented me as the class cheater. I was so humiliated and so shocked that I couldn't speak. She sent me out of the class as a warning to any other student who might be tempted to cheat.

How I dreaded reporting my miserable experience to my mother. My parents didn't need another burden. They had so little and worked so hard in those days just to keep food on the table, but they always gave their love and attention to each of us in abundance. How I hated to disappoint them!

I was sure that when my mother heard about what happened to me in class, she would not be sympathetic. She was more apt to assume I was in the wrong … and she knew for sure that I chattered too much. I decided to put off my confession, but she knew something had happened and demanded that I tell her the bad news. After I tearfully told her the story, all she said was, "Did you cheat on that test?" I told her "no, we were just talking." "Then, get ready for bed and we'll talk about it in the morning."

THE DAY MY MOTHER STOOD UP FOR ME

The next morning I told her I couldn't go back to school. She assured me that I could … and would … and she would walk to school with me. She wouldn't be dissuaded and I didn't know she could walk so fast! On arrival, she walked down the hall straight to Mrs. Simpson's class and to her desk where my mother invited the teacher out in the hall. I was standing out by the lockers but I clearly heard her say, "You accused my daughter of cheating in front of the whole class. She has told me that she didn't cheat and I believe her. I want Betty out of your class today."

With that she turned toward the Principal's office with me in tow. My mother rescued me. She revived my self esteem. She believed in me and did something about it!

Betty and her mother

Sisterhood

Mothers, Daughters, Sisters and Girlfriends ... the threads that hold the fabric of life together ... at least that is what I have experienced. We "girls" share many of the same emotions, dreams, joys and sorrows. There are many times through the years when only another woman can understand or really even care how we feel.

I believe the need for "sisters" begins at our mother's breast and grows even stronger with the birth of a younger sister, continuing into school days when we discover other girls our own age are experiencing the same wonders and the same problems we are experiencing.

I was so blessed to have a loving mother who loved me unconditionally and who looked to God for her strength through some very hard years. My two younger sisters, Shirley and Eleanore were my best friends. We played and cried together. Sometimes we fought, but always settled our disputes before sundown. What choice did we have? We were sisters! This unique female relationship only became stronger when I had my first daughter. I felt that it was she and I against the world! In 1948 when my second daughter, Melinda, came into my life, I witnessed that same female bond grow so tightly between the two sisters. During the years 1950—1954, while my children were in the Wichita Children's Home, Melody took over as mother to her baby sister. How glad I am that they had this close relationship while I couldn't be there!

Melinda was probably hurt more than any of the children during this period because she was only eighteen months old when she was taken with her siblings to the home. She missed out on being "mothered" through those early years with the cuddling and rocking chair moments that the other children had experienced and could still remember.

SISTERHOOD

After I became able to move all of them back into our little house, Melinda loved having a room with her big sister. She especially enjoyed "collections" which she shared with Melody, particularly her rock collections secretly stored under their bed. Her two brothers found her a great target for their teasing. Unfortunately, she took their teasing much too seriously. When Hank joined the family, he discouraged this boyish activity, becoming Melinda's strongest ally and protector. She needed him so much in her life ... the first father she had ever known!

All through elementary school and junior high, Melinda always had to have a "best friend" and her delight was to serve them her favorite, "donuts and Kool-Aid," in our basement playroom! She, fortunately, had a couple of years to be the baby of her new family and to learn that she did have a special place in that unit. In 1962 she shared my secret of the new baby's coming with Melody and owned the event so much that she told her dad, "Hank, I know John is your baby, but I think he's mostly mother's because she had him." Hank was too wise to argue with that assumption! She and Johnny moved to Alaska with us in the summer of 1965 and lived on base at Elmendorf Air Force Base. John was enrolled in the base nursery school and Melinda finished senior high school in Anchorage. She attended college at Kansas State University in Manhattan, Kansas, where she lived with her then married sister and brother-in-law. Melody was teaching English in Adult Education and Richard was beginning his profession as an architect. One day I got a phone call from Melody that she had made Melinda quit college because she wasn't applying herself and had one too many "woodsies" (college parties) and was missing school. When Melody knew the facts, she felt she had to act on them. In her words to Melinda, "it isn't right for you to spend the folks' money for college when you are cutting classes." I think Melinda was relieved, as she really wasn't interested in higher education at that time. She got a job and worked for the rest of the year.

The next few years saw her married to a Navy officer and proudly producing two outstanding sons, Darron and Derek. The family made their home in Washington State and later in Ventura, California, which was fortunate for us. We were able to see the boys grow up to become very successful men

in their own right. Darron is a Realtor in Southern California, and Derek is a Radiologist at a University hospital in New York City.

Melinda is a woman of unusual talent, insight and accomplishment. She is the Broker/Owner of a residential real estate company in Newport Beach, California and does a lot of compassionate community work herself! Like her mother, she's had to learn some things the hard way, but she has never forgotten her roots and those people she loves and respects. When I think back on the life she inherited, I am very sad that I couldn't have made it better for her baby years. She is my precious baby daughter who has become my **only** daughter. Now we can share, woman-to-woman, our views past and present without apology and without regret. We love getting together and can laugh at things we used to resent. As Melinda would say to any girl who would use mistakes or humble beginnings as excuses, "Get over it. Life is too short!"

Betty and precious daughter Melinda

I would advise all girls to treasure the women in your life. As you mature you will find that most of the time, it is a woman, whether from your own family members or those special "sister-friends" who will cry with you through your heartbreaks and rejoice with you in your successes.

SISTERHOOD

Special "sisters-friends" with Betty.
Anita Mackey - top left
Rochelle Rose - top right
Patricia Montemayor - bottom left
Helen Jepsen - lower right

THE CARPENTER'S DAUGHTER

They Called Me a Rat!

"A True Fable"

One thing for sure, I should never have left my mother! It was such a beautiful day out in the meadow, I just thought I'd explore a little bit. It didn't take me long to run across a big ditch where rain water went through. Water would have stopped me but it was very dry that day. I hopped through a hole in a fence, went up a little hill and there was the softest, greenest grass I'd ever seen. At the top of the hill was a yellow building with a little red house behind it.

I stopped for a minute and wondered what to do next. I knew I wanted to see what was inside the yellow building. It looked welcoming enough, but how could I get in? I

The screamin' female saw me first. She looked me right in the eye and started hollering, "Hank, there he is ... there's the rat!"

went to the far corner of the building, up on a red deck and saw the sun sparkling on the glass pane. I felt really lucky to find it open with just enough room to squeeze through! What a surprise!!

There were pretty colors all around with wooden objects against the wall. I thought I would take a look around and maybe find something good to eat. I went up a couple of little steps into another room just minding my own business when a tall creature started screaming "Help ... Hank, it's a rat ... come quick!"

It sounded like a female creature ... and she was up on some kind of ledge or seat screaming her head off ... "it's a rat ... it's a rat!" She was pointing right at me and I was scared.

The next thing I heard was an even bigger creature come into the room, the one she called "Hank," I guess. He never did see me, but said, "It's more afraid of you, Betty, than you are of him. I'll put some cheese in a trap." Oh, Goody, I thought ... maybe that's something to eat. Maybe this Hank creature is more reasonable than the screamer!

They Called Me a Rat!

By this time it was beginning to get dark and I wanted to get away from the bright lights. They hurt my eyes and I don't need any light to see where I'm going. I headed back into another area with no lights on and slipped through an open door with shiny glass where I settled down among some shoes and boxes. I waited until the creatures quieted down. I could hear them in the big room with music playing. After awhile I thought, "I need to get out of here and let them see how nice I am so they won't call me a 'rat'." So, I walked out into the open doorway and just stood there looking as sweet and kind as I knew how. The screamin' female saw me first. She looked me right in the eye and started hollering, "Hank, there he is … there's the rat!" I wasn't even given a chance to be friendly. I'm not sure that I'm more afraid of them than they are of me!! I backed up slowly, then scampered back among the shoes. I stayed there until I fell asleep.

The next morning I heard the creatures scurrying around early, carrying things outside, back and forth until it became very quiet. I figured they'd left the building, so I came out of hiding and did some exploring. I found the cheese in a couple of wooden blocks that snapped when I got the cheese. If I'd had a smaller head, it might have been cut off! I crawled up on a big counter where water comes out … boy, for this job you really need my long claws! I can hang on to any slick surface and go all the way to the top. Anyway, on top of this counter I saw a bright yellow plant that looked like it might be good to eat. It was long and curved with a covering I had to peel back, but boy was the stuff inside good. I ate it all but the peeling.

The next three days inside this prison were not so good. There was no more cheese and no more long fruit that I could find and it was even hard for me to sleep among the shoes, I got so hungry. Well, the fourth day I heard all the noise and knew the creatures were back. They instantly saw the mess I'd made with broken glass and my droppings throughout the house. Well, I couldn't help it … they shouldn't have left me hungry and defenseless for so long. The she-creature started hollering, "It's the rat … look what he's done!" She became completely hysterical and believe me, I was plenty tired of being called a rat. No rat could have climbed the heights I climbed or covered the territory I covered while the creatures were gone. At least, I don't just run around the walls and I have a much prettier face and very expressive eyes.

Well, after the screaming I retreated again to the place the shoes were and I heard both exit doors close. Now, I was really trapped! I was up all night trying to find an escape but there just wasn't any. The next morning while I was trying to sleep behind a big piece of furniture, I heard a third creature come in with, "Mom, you've put up with this rat long enough. I'm going to get rid of it for you." "Oh, thank goodness," the screamer answered. "I haven't had a peaceful moment for over five days." She called the new creature "Randy" and it was pretty obvious that he was out for bear! He was instructing the screamer to help him make a tunnel of cushions and furniture that led from my area to the outside. I heard a lot of movement in the main room, then Randy said, "Now I'm going to open the bedroom door." I guess that's where I was. "You hold this broom and urge the rat on through the tunnel."

By this time the screamer, with her broom club was up on top of something, hollering, "Don't let him come over my way!" as if anyone would want to come her way. Randy came close to where I was. He rumbled around in all the shoes, but luckily, I wasn't there. Then he started pulling out heavy furniture and finally got too close for comfort, so I did what any smart possum would do. I acted like I was dead!

The next thing I heard was Randy, when he discovered my poor body, say "Mom, it's not a rat, it's just a baby possum." Well, I'm no baby, more like a teenager, but I was scared. Then I felt a gloved hand grab hold of my beautiful long tail and hold me up over a trash can, walking hurriedly out the front door. The screamer tried to take a picture of me, but Randy was moving so fast, she didn't get much. I'll say something for Randy. He had compassion and he didn't seem to be afraid or dislike possums. He let me dangle by my tail, trying my best to get my claws up to get loose, to no avail.

He went around the house down the grassy hill and put me over the fence in the same field I had come through a few days before. In just seconds he turned me loose and I was off to find my mother! Wait 'til she hears about how I was treated. "Rat, indeed," she'll say. "Don't those creatures know we are from the noble lineage of O'possums?"

POEMS FROM MY HEART

Melody

You were mother's first love
Describe how I feel?
I still find it hard
To believe that you're real!
Dark eyes that sparkle,
Little turned-up nose,
Talking hands and dancing toes.
Sweet and cuddly,
But ready to fight,
Your bubbling laughter
Is my secret delight.
I think of that day
God gave you to me,
My life wrote it's song
With my "Melody."

Michael

You've often been called my favorite son,
I won't deny this, you truly are one!
More pride in a son a mom never had,
I counted on you when you were only a lad.
A dreamer of song, with no time for tears
Your infectious smile dispels all my fears.
A romantic at heart, you give it your best,
Do more than your part, let love do the rest!
I named you "Michael" meaning "like God."
May He ever be near you as life's paths you trod.

Randy

The cutest little guy, a regular boy,
Affectionate, happy – a mother's pure joy,
A charmer through school, a leader at play
With a fiery temper that's still with you today.
By nature you're shy, you feel best at home.
With the right woman's touch, you're not apt to roam
I'm proud of the boy and the man that you are.
I believe in your dreams hitched high to a star.
"Randy" means "warrior", but braver are you,
Who lives by the words, "To thine own self be true."

Melinda

Melinda means gentle and gentle are you
From your dimpled toes to your eyes of blue.
So little you ask from life, my dear,
Just to have someone you love very near.
Perhaps it's because you've so much to share
Your own special way of saying "I care."
Have I been blind or could it be
Those hidden hopes inside of me
Reflected in you from God above?
Melinda Sue, my child of love!

John

Diddle diddle dumpling, our son, John
We'll never forget the day you were born.
Like a chubby papoose one wanted to squeeze.
Uniquely packaged, designed to please!
Born to parents "over the hill,"
You called us "you guys" and gave us our fill
Of Little League to college baseball scores.
But never neglecting your studies or chores.
Your fine sense of humor, your religious cause,
Your dependable love gives your family pause
To reflect on God's blessing to make us the ones
To be blessed with a son whom we call John!

The Belly Laugh

How long's it been since your reserve gave way
To a belly laugh, remember the day?
When a serious moment couldn't hold in
The tears of laughter, your audible grin?
It doesn't happen nearly often enough.
If it did, life's road wouldn't be so tough.
The best laughing subject, I find is me
When I don't take myself too seriously!
It's funny out there. … a frame of mind
Look around, look up, I think you'll find
A smile, a chuckle, a joke in the making
A belly laugh waiting, just for the taking!

Grandchildren
Back Row: Dustin, Joseph, Danny
Middle Row: Betty, Hank, Shawn
Front Row: Derek, Jannelle, Darron

His Only Son

My joy at his birth I'll never forget
I had little to give him on earth, and yet
I knew somehow that life had begun
When I looked in the face of my newborn son.

I was there when he sang his first childish song.
I heard his prayers when he confessed a wrong.
We walked thro' woods and fished small streams
We laughed together and shared big dreams!

I can still feel the squeeze of his little hands
The trust that made me a bigger man.
One wonderful moment I shared with my wife,
The day Tommy gave the Lord his life.

The Father's business he had to do
A special calling that comes to few.
He belonged to others, He always had,
But I was chosen to be his dad!

Tommy, my son, it's time to go
To the care of One you already know
God feels the hurt your leaving has done
He gave His only Begotten Son.

You live again and we will too
It won't be long 'til I'll be with you.
We'll walk through woods and fish small streams
We'll laugh together and share big dreams!

(Written for my Dad at the death of his only son, Rev. Tom R. Pyeatt in 1968.)

Last Waltz on the Danube

Two shadows are one, 'gainst a soft summer sky
How often we've glided, so close you and I.
From sea to the mountains, our love knows the flight
We laughed in the sunlight, were one in the night.

Sweet songs speak of longing, as I hold you so near,
The soft Danube whispers, "I love you, my dear."
The sounds of our waltz, with the waves rolled away
The touch of your hand said you wanted to stay.

But the Danube had beckoned, I knew by your smile
That we must be parted for a little while.
Sounds never cease and the waves are returning,
My heart beats a rhythm of infinite yearning.

Sleep on, my sweet Prince, the days are but few,
'Til I shall dance the last waltz with you!

(Written on a Russian cruise ship in August, 1984, cruising down the Danube to
the Black Sea. On board was an elegant German couple from Vienna who danced
together so gracefully. One evening during a gala party, he collapsed, never to
regain consciousness. I wrote this poem for his widow.)

Gate of Hope

The line is forming outside the gate
Some came for food,
Some for relief from solitude,
Hope and longing for something more?
Maybe this time will open a door.
The evening's cool — with smoke in the air
But different somehow from anywhere.
All around the Mission grounds,
Sweet music and prayer in the Chapel sounds.
I don't want to hear that Story, you know.
Just feed me my fill and let me go.
In my rags of despair, I expect no more,
Let's get this line moving and open the door!
My wife is long gone … my children don't know me.
It's just as well, 'cause I want to be free.
Yeah, free? That's a laugh, as I stand here in chains
Of troubles and demons that fight for my brains.
The sun's going down under the cross,
Standing high above the gate,
Is there room for me in your kingdom, God?
Or do you think I've waited too late?
Maybe tonight I'll hear your Word
While waiting for one more meal
Can I really believe your Son died for me?
That the love of God is real?
Don't let go of my hand, Dear Lord
Open my heart as I wait.
Maybe I'll find the answers this time
Just inside the gate.

(Written for the Santa Barbara Rescue Mission)

John 14
Christ's Great Promise

by Betty Rosness

Every Ninety Days Something Else Falls Off

When I was young, be-freckled, and skinny
Old age never entered my mind
My stamina was endless like the energy bunny
Each day a new mountain to climb

In my twenties, thirties, and forties it's true
I sailed through most storms with ease
My life could only get better and better
From day to day was a breeze

I reached my peak around age fifty-five
Every year brought a new plateau
Around seventy-nine changes began to arrive
More ways than you want to know

A broken ankle slowed my pace
By eighty, Bells Palsy attacked my face
One side up, the other side down
My near perfect smile was a crooked frown

One brow loomed lower than the other
Facial nerves had damaged my speech
About that time I would discover
Youthful properties were out of my reach

With my cane in hand I now cripple
To places where I used to run
I smile with my eyes and a dimple
And act like I'm having fun

My skinny body has begun to swell
The skin has a noticeable sag
Well meaning friends say "You're looking well"
While I feel like an old dishrag

There aren't enough concealers to cover the dents
Nor pencils to fill in the lines
Thank God I still have my Opium Scent
To cover the sign of the times

Look up wise friends … all is not lost
Dear youths, listen up less you scoff
There will be a day when you'll count the cost
When every ninety days something else falls off

Betty and Hank on Hank's 90th birthday - 2009

EPILOGUE

TIME has an uncanny way of putting life's harshest pain and assaults in their proper dimension. Choices are so very important and as we make those choices we must be willing to own them with the consequences they produce. With all the advantages I was born with: loving parents of character, a strong spiritual heritage, good health, and more than my share of God-given gifts, I have often wondered how I could have made the choices I made. However, when I look at the whole picture, I must admit that I wouldn't have missed the ability and opportunity to love without reservation. I could never imagine life without knowing the four extraordinary children resulting from my misplaced love.

Though my children's father passed away in 1994, I have always prayed for him to find forgiveness and peace in life here and for eternity. His children have inherited his physical good looks and his artistic talent. His five grandsons carry those qualities into another generation. No, I am not sorry that I loved him too much, nor that I reconciled with him countless times and married him twice! At times I didn't want to live, but I did and have had a fabulous life. I learned a lot through the tears. I know now that love is a two-person challenge and can be destroyed forever if not nurtured.

Through all the rough times, I asked God to keep me from bitterness and He did! Once I knew for sure that there was no hope for a life with my first love, I never looked back. The step by step journey to make it on my own made me stronger, more confident and more creative. The harder I worked and the closer I got to my goal, the more energy I had.

I'd like to say that I always followed the narrow way, but there was a period that I felt that being sweet and trusting hadn't worked for me and that I needed to learn how life as a young, cast-off mother could really be. As a woman, I needed affirmation that I was desirable and I found there were plenty of young men out there to help in that quest. I was looking for real love in all the wrong places with people as miserable

THE CARPENTER'S DAUGHTER

as I had become. During that period I constantly begged God "please don't let go of my hand."

I truly believe it was because of the prayers of my parents and Christian friends that I came though that period with all four of my children, my health, and my faith in God. I had truly been through the fire and through it all was becoming a vessel fit to be a contributing child of God.

In my career and in my soon to be fifty year marriage, I've learned that the most important ingredient to inner peace and happiness is understanding and practicing FORGIVENESS. I believe we need to forgive even when we're not asked for forgiveness; forgive when the offense is "unforgivable;" and FORGIVE injuries we can never forget. God forgives us unconditionally. We have only to ask Him with sincere repentance. With His help we can forgive anything. We can never truly move forward in life or realize our full potential while holding a grudge or hate in our hearts.

I feel so blessed that love truly rules my life … love for my husband, my children, my friends, my country, the lonely, the outcasts, the despondent, and the sick. If the things that have happened in my life gave me compassion and love for all these, then I'm glad they happened. For this reason I have few regrets, only thanksgiving for the ability to care so much.

To all who read these words,
I wish you true love.
Embrace love when
you find it
and never be afraid
to let it show!!

ALWAYS, *Betty*